Understanding the Scriptures

LOWELL L. BENNION

Deseret Book Company
Salt Lake City, Utah
1981

© 1981 Deseret Book Company
Printed in the United States of America
All rights reserved
First printing April 1981
Library of Congress Catalog Card Number 81-66422
ISBN 0-87747-863-5

Contents

Preface

George Bernard Shaw said the Bible is a wonderful book because you can prove anything you wish by it. What he says is quite true if you pick and choose isolated passages and incidents. Shakespeare stated the practice with his usual aptness:

In religion,
What damned error, but some sober brow
Will bless it, and approve it with a text
Hiding the grossness with fair ornament?
    —Merchant of Venice, *act 3, sc. 2*

In this book I shall present some guidelines that I believe should be kept in mind as we read scripture, if we are to interpret it fairly and with understanding. Scriptures are unique books and cannot be read intelligently unless their distinctive character and intent are understood.

Some parts of scripture are so clear and simple that a child can gain much from them. Other portions are so obscure and difficult that mature minds have difficulty understanding them. A friend of mine was called to preside over a German-speaking mission. To recover his German after a forty-year absence from the mission field, he began reading the Book of Mormon in German. He did quite well, he said, until he came to chapters quoted from Isaiah. To solve his problem, he turned to the book of Isaiah in his native English Bible and confessed, "I didn't understand the writings of Isaiah any better in English than I had done in German." It is the intent of this work to help the reader understand the scriptures.

I enjoy the scriptures. Each time I read or teach one of the standard works, I discover ideas, questions, and relationships that I had never noticed before. The books are the same ones that I read thirty or forty years ago, but I am not the same person. Things have happened to me in the meantime so that I bring a new perspective to my reading. Words don't convey meanings so much as they call them forth. Reading is an active, creative relationship between the author and the reader. This is why we can return to the same great books again and again and find them new and refreshing.

Years ago, while teaching religion to college students, I became acutely aware of their need to know how to study scripture. To meet this need, I developed some brief guidelines that were printed as Appendix B in *Religion and Pursuit of Truth* (Deseret Book Co., 1959). With the present added emphasis in the Church on reading the scriptures, there is an even greater need for guidance in this pleasant undertaking. For this reason I have expanded this earlier, brief effort into this book.

This work is intended primarily for those interested in the standard works of the Latter-day Saint faith. Much of what follows applies also to the scriptures of other world religions, but to keep this work within reasonable bounds, its application has been confined to the four scriptures of The Church of Jesus Christ of Latter-day Saints: the Bible, Book of Mormon, Doctrine and Covenants, and Pearl of Great Price.

My thanks go to my students who have led me to deeper appreciation of scripture as we have studied together. Thanks also to generous critics Emma Lou Thayne, Hermana Lyon, Edith Shepherd, Keith Eddington, Lowell C. Bennion, and Mary L. Bradford, who have read and critiqued the manuscript and thereby spared me errors and ambiguity. My appreciation goes to Ellen B. Stone for multiple typings and editing. I also appreciate the suggestions and fine cooperation of Lowell M. Durham, Jr. and the staff of the Deseret Book Company. I alone remain responsible for the ideas expressed.

1

The Distinctive Character
of Scripture

Scriptures differ from other books in several ways. No volume of scripture is a single unified work of one author written at a given time to a particular audience. Each is a collection of writings produced over centuries or decades by many writers, not all of them known. Even the Doctrine and Covenants, which now covers over 150 years, has several authors and was written under varying circumstances in diverse places from New York State to Utah. These separate writings, written as single works, were later brought together as the Bible, the Book of Mormon, the Doctrine and Covenants, and the Pearl of Great Price.

The scriptures are as diversified in content as they are in makeup. This is particularly true of the Old Testament, which contains history, narration, songs, prayers, parables, genealogies, codes of conduct, exhortation, prophecies, poetry, and a dramatic debate. In addition to revelations, the Doctrine and Covenants contains historical accounts, declarations of beliefs, prophecies, sermons, epistles, and minutes of meetings.

With the exception of the Doctrine and Covenants and part of the Pearl of Great Price, the scriptures have come to English readers in translation from Hebrew, Greek, and Reformed Egyptian. Like any work of translation, they have suffered in the process. For example, since Joseph Smith was not a literary scholar and writer as were the translators of the King James Bible, the Book of Mormon may suffer somewhat in language and style because it is a literal translation of a tongue very foreign to English.

Another unique feature of the scriptures is that they come to us as the word of God. Many writings of men and women through the ages may have been inspired of God, but many authors of scripture knew they were speaking for him. Micah, for example, declared, "But truly I am full of power by the spirit of the Lord, and of judgment, and of might, to declare unto Jacob his transgression, and to Israel his sin." (Micah 3:8.)

And Amos justified his words in this wise to the high priest Amaziah, who told him to flee home to Judah and not to prophesy against Israel: "I was no prophet, neither was I a prophet's son; but I was an herdman, and a gatherer of sycomore fruit: And the Lord took me as I followed the flock, and the Lord said unto me, Go, prophesy unto my people Israel. Now therefore hear thou the word of the Lord." (Amos 7:14-16.)

For believers, this divine sanction of scripture gives it an authoritative status not accorded other books that must win their way strictly on their own merit as judged by their readers.

What do we mean when we say that the Book of Mormon is the word of God, or that the Bible is the word of God as far as it is translated correctly? This statement has different meanings for different people. Some believers in the Bible as the word of God hold that every word and every verse are equally sacrosanct, pure dictation from Deity. Others believe that God is capable of better language than that found in scripture. Some cannot understand how the same God could have inspired such different ethical standards as are found in parts of the law of Moses and the ideals of Christ in the New Testament. We must consider what it really means to call scripture the word of God.

We cannot read scripture as we would any other book if we would understand and appreciate it. The purpose of this book is to provide perspective on the nature of scripture and to suggest some basic concepts to keep in mind as we read scripture, and, it is hoped, to increase our understanding and enjoyment.

Some readers may think it presumptuous of me—after all, I am neither a prophet nor a son of a prophet—to comment on holy writ. It is said that scripture is not "of private interpretation" and that when elders speak, "whatsoever they shall speak when moved upon by the Holy Ghost shall be scripture, shall be the will of the Lord, shall be the mind of the Lord, shall be the word of the Lord, shall be the voice of the Lord, and the power of God unto salvation." (D&C 68:4.)

In response, may I say that I am not so much interpreting scripture as suggesting helps when we do seek to interpret it. This we all do whenever we read, teach, or preach the word of God. This is done in every course of study. Words and sentences have no meaning until someone gives meaning to them. There is no alternative. We must interpret scripture to discover its meaning.

The scriptures have won my affection and allegiance not only because they are the standard works of my church and because I have learned to treat them as such, but because of their inherent worth—their rich human experience, their truths, their beautiful language, and their inspiration. Despite their diversity of authorship and of time and place of origin, they are unified by their authors' common search for truth, for God, and for the meaning and values of life. The reader who shares these same interests will also gain a feeling of unity and cohesiveness as he reads the scriptures.

The scriptures, as we shall see, are not abstract works of science, philosophy, or theology. They are a record of life—of man's failures and sins, goodness and righteousness, fears and faith, as seen and evaluated by authors inspired of God. They are indeed a unique legacy worthy of our earnest and continued study.

2

The Background and Makeup
of Scripture

The scriptures were written neither in heaven nor in a vacuum. They were created by prophets and other authors who lived at specific times and places in human history. The writers of scripture were addressing real men and women about problems and issues of deep concern. For example, Moses spoke to the Israelites as he led them along the tortuous road from Egyptian bondage to the borders of Canaan where they had to fight their way into the promised land, a people one step removed from idolatry and ever tempted to step back into it.

Amos (765 B.C.) spoke to the northern kingdom of Israel at a time when there were marked class distinctions between rich and poor and when men gained wealth by removing landmarks, falsifying weights and measures, selling people into slavery for the price of a pair of shoes, taking bribes in the courts, oppressing the widow and the orphan, and having no compassion for the afflicted in Israel. Amos came at a time when the nation of Israel could easily be conquered by the great power of Assyria. He was bent on saving his people from corruption and thereby gaining Jehovah's intervention against the might of Assyria.

The apostle Paul preached the Gospel first to the Jews in the Roman Empire and then to the Gentiles. His was a twofold task—first to convert Jews to Christianity as he had been converted, then to convert to the Christian faith and ethical standards gentiles steeped in Greek learning and worldly life-styles.

Moses, Amos, and Paul spoke and wrote in the context of their day about their culture and the living conditions of their respective peoples. Occasionally they looked ahead to a later date, to predict the long-range consequences of the actions of their peoples. Sometimes they had visions of hope, of a golden age when Israel, or at least a remnant thereof, would be redeemed—when the lamb and the lion would lie down together, when men would beat their swords into plowshares and would learn war no more. (Isaiah 2:4.) Their prophetic statements are greatly enhanced if we appreciate the painful, discouraging circumstances that gave them birth. Think of Moroni—the lone survivor of the Nephites—who, having seen his whole beloved nation perish, looked forward to the coming forth of his record to bless both Lamanites and Gentiles.

When General Authorities speak to the Saints today, they also speak at a definite place and at a definite time to people they know. And they talk about things that concern them today. They speak in the light of age-old gospel principles and perspectives, but the applications are contemporary. A person unacquainted with the climate of opinion and conditions of today would not understand them. Prophets of old likewise were enmeshed in their times and cultures even as our leaders are today.

The scriptures were not written in the Salt Lake City or London or Frankfurt or Sydney of today. They were written centuries ago in other lands and cultures and, for the most part, in different languages. This adds to their interest and value. But if we would understand them, we must try to put ourselves in the position of the writers and the people to whom they wrote. Admittedly this is difficult, but any knowledge we gain of the history, language, and culture of scriptural peoples will enhance our understanding and appreciation of their records.

Although written in another time and place, scriptures contain much that is valid for us today. This is true because human nature over time and across cultures changes little. Religious principles have lasting and universal application. Then too, as surely as men speak under the influence of the Holy Spirit, they will speak that which is good and true and usually valid for all seasons.

If one reads the scriptures with some perspective on the origin and background of a particular work, he will be better able to distinguish between fundamental doctrine and true ethical principles on the one hand, and, on the other, practices, policies, and exhortations that are best suited for particular periods of time and conditions. Not everything in scripture is normative or standard for us today. The whole sacrificial system of the law of Moses was done away with by the mission of Christ. (3 Nephi 9:17.) Certain hygienic and dietary rules of the law of Moses that had meaning for ancient Israel are no longer useful today.

Changing conditions call for changes in religious organization and practice. We do not expect innovation in such basic principles as the Ten Commandments, the Beatitudes, first principles and ordinances, or doctrines of Deity and man. But there have been and will continue to be changes in many other policies and practices that will better serve the theology and ethical teachings of the gospel. In 1890 The Church of Jesus Christ of Latter-day Saints ceased the practice of polygamy in the United States, and in 1904 everywhere else. Blacks received access to the priesthood in 1978. The full First Quorum of the Seventy is being implemented. A system of Regional Representatives has been established to meet the administrative needs of a rapidly growing, international church. Other changes in policy and practices will come when needed, as inspired and confirmed by revelation.

Religion is not a static legal document produced once and for all time, complete and unalterable. Rather it has come to us from "God, who at sundry times and in divers manners spake in time past unto the fathers by the prophets, Hath in these last days spoken unto us by his Son." (Hebrews 1:1-2.) And, since the days of Christ, he has spoken and will continue to speak to his prophets as they seek and need him.

To appreciate more fully the scriptures—the most authentic record we have of religion—we need to study them in their historical, geographical, and cultural settings.

The Makeup of Scripture

I have heard people say with considerable pride and satisfaction that they have read the Bible from cover to cover. Their pride is understandable, since the Bible is long and difficult reading. But to read it from cover to cover may not be the most sensible way to study the Bible, especially the Old Testament. The Old Testament is, after all, not a single work, but a collection of thirty-nine separate writings. It should be thought of more as a shelf of books that editors centuries later placed between two covers. In doing so, they did not always use chronological order or logical arrangement.

To appreciate the Bible and other scriptures, one should read each writing within any scripture as a separate book. Books similar in purpose and chronology should be read as a group. The importance of this approach can be illustrated with the Old Testament.

The Old Testament

The Jews divided the Old Testament—their sacred canon of scripture—into three categories: the Law, the Prophets, and the Writings. The Law embraced the first five books of the Bible: Genesis, Exodus, Leviticus, Numbers, and Deuteronomy. Ascribed to Moses,[1] they

---

[1]Martin Luther's Bible calls them I Mose, II Mose, III Mose, IV Mose, and V Mose.

have been authoritative and sacred for orthodox Jews through the centuries. These five books contain not only laws and rules of conduct, they also tell the dramatic and heroic epic stories of the founding fathers and recount historical events that brought Israel into being as a nation and people.

The second group of Old Testament books, called the Prophets, contains books of narration: Joshua, Judges, 1 and 2 Samuel, 1 and 2 Kings, and fifteen prophetic books. The books written by or about the prophets such as Amos, Hosea, Isaiah, Micah, Jeremiah, and Jonah are among the greatest of all scriptural writings from the point of view of their teachings and their literary power and beauty. These books need to be rearranged chronologically and placed in their historical settings. (See chapter 10.)

The remaining Old Testament books are called the Writings. Prominent among them is the wisdom literature: Proverbs, Ecclesiastes, and Job. The famous and delightful stories of Ruth and Esther also belong here, as do the Psalms. The Writings were not collected and made part of the Jewish canon until about A.D. 150. This is illustrated by an incident in the Gospels. A young lawyer asked Jesus: "Master, which is the great commandment in the law?" Unhesitatingly Jesus answered, the love of God and the love of neighbor. Then he said, "On these two commandments hang all the law and the prophets." (Matthew 22:36-40.) Why did Jesus not say, "On these two commandments hang all the law and the prophets and the writings"? The answer is simple—the Writings, while in existence, had not been canonized into scripture in Jesus' day.

To read the Old Testament with the greatest understanding, one should rearrange the books therein both in chronological and in a logical sequence. This has been done in the last chapters of this book as an introduction to each of the four standard works.

3

The Authors of Scripture

The various writers of scripture are not alike. Some were prophets of God who spoke with authority and conviction and gave us great truths. Others were unnamed and unknown. Still others were successors, sons of former writers, who wrote to continue the record. This is especially true of the Book of Mormon.

In the Old Testament we do not know who was the final writer or editor of the first five books or of Joshua, Judges, 1 and 2 Samuel, 1 and 2 Kings, 1 and 2 Chronicles, Jonah, Job, and many others. Ecclesiastes, although ascribed to Solomon, was written much later and by another hand. The Psalms were written not only by David but also by songwriters over centuries of Israelite history. Some were written while the Jews were in exile in Babylon. Proverbs is a collection of writings based on much of Israelite history—a far richer work than Solomon could have produced by himself. No one knows who wrote Daniel, Ezra, Nehemiah, or the Song of Solomon.

What should we conclude from the nature of the authorship of the Bible? I would suggest two things. First, the writings of the great prophets of Israel and of Paul, James, and John and other known men of the New Testament are likely to be more authoritative expressions of doctrine and the will of God and Christ than are works of narration, of history, and of practical wisdom by unknown authors. I much prefer, for example, the book of Amos to that of the Song of Solomon. I read Job, Ecclesiastes, and Proverbs for their wisdom and beauty of language, but not as doctrinal treatises.

I would also suggest that the important question, in the last analysis, is not the author of a given book, but what does it contain of value, inspiration, and profit? An unknown author can be just as inspired as anyone else. Job is a profound book of unexcelled literary quality. Jonah teaches great truths concerning God's universal influence, his justice and mercy. Yet the authors of Jonah and Job are unknown.

Most of the New Testament was written by apostles and disciples of Christ who were relatively close to the events and times they record. New Testament books, therefore, are consistently more authentic and in a sense more authoritative than a number of books in the Old Testament. The expanse of history covered in the Old Testament, however, makes it richer, in some respects, than the New Testament.

The Book of Mormon record was kept over centuries by successive authors whose writings vary in quantity and lasting significance. Chemish, for example, confesses a faithful but small writing effort: "Now I, Chemish, write what few things I write, in the same book with my brother; for behold, I saw the last which he wrote, that he wrote it with his own hand; and he wrote it in the day that he delivered them unto me. And after this manner we keep the records, for it is according to the commandments of our fathers. And I make an end." (Omni 9.)

Despite the multiple authorship of the Book of Mormon, it conveys a sense of unity to the reader because it is largely the abridgment of a single author, Mormon, and a single translator, Joseph Smith. Even so, original writers such as Nephi, Jacob, Alma, and Moroni make substantial and original contributions.

Even though scriptures were inspired of God, they

were written by men of flesh and blood, men who had distinctive minds of their own. The ones we know—such as Amos, Isaiah, Paul, Alma, Joseph Smith—were men of strong character. Their personalities, as well as the influence of Deity, are reflected in their writings. We should give credit to authors as well as to God for what we revere as holy writ.

Latter-day Saints should have learned from their own experience that prophets of God speak for him "at sundry times and in divers manners." Joseph Smith, Brigham Young, John Taylor, Wilford Woodruff, Lorenzo Snow, Joseph F. Smith, Heber J. Grant, George Albert Smith, David O. McKay, Joseph Fielding Smith, Harold B. Lee, and Spencer W. Kimball all have spoken with power from on high, but each has had his own style, his unique emphasis. Prophets of God are not puppets; they are more than tape recorders. They speak for themselves as well as for God. Under divine influence they rise to unusual heights, but they are not infallible, nor do they cease to be human beings. Joseph Smith wrote that he was visited by "a brother and sister from Michigan who thought that 'a prophet is always a prophet;' but [he] told them that a prophet was a prophet only when he was acting as such." (History of the Church 5:265.)

Writers of scripture vary in their ability to interpret the will of God, in their receptivity to his Spirit, in their need for certain kinds of revelation. Joseph Smith, for example, received numerous new revelations on Church doctrine, organization, ritual, and religious conduct because he sensed so strongly that these things needed to be restored, and because God responded to his need and questions. A vacuum of knowledge existed in the budding Church. Likewise, in establishing the religion and nation of Israel, Moses had great need for abundant explicit revelation. Jesus has given us the highest and finest interpretation of the gospel because of his noble and divine nature and because of his intimate relationship to the Father. He becomes the ultimate standard for those of us who profess Christian discipleship.

4

Correctness of Translation

"We believe the Bible to be the word of God as far as it is translated correctly; we also believe the Book of Mormon to be the word of God." (Article of Faith 8.)

The Bible, Book of Mormon, and parts of the Pearl of Great Price have come to English-speaking people only in translation. All four standard works are known to most people in non-English-speaking lands only in translation. Great writing often suffers in translation. Anyone who knows Shakespeare in English and then reads him in German, and likewise anyone who knows Goethe in German and then reads him in English, senses the loss of some beauty and meaning.

To gain full and accurate understanding of scripture, then, we would need to know the original languages—Hebrew, Aramaic, Greek, Reformed Egyptian, and English. Since this is beyond the capacity and ambition of most of us, what should we do? What is the next best?

Next best is to review the work of scholars who have been or are acquainted with the original languages. This includes contemporary researchers, because our knowledge of ancient languages and cultures increases over time. Even learned men can be biased and in error. To guard against this, I suggest we compare the work of a number of reputable scholars. As I read various Bible translations, I generally find minor differences and nuances, but essential agreement of basic ideas among translators. It is interesting also to compare the Bible in two or more modern languages. Luther, for example, produced a beautiful Bible in German that gave great impetus to the eventual creation of a national language of "high" German.

Latter-day Saints can also compare Joseph Smith's revision with other translations. The Prophet recognized that there were mistranslations in the Bible, and he sought, through inspiration and revelation, to correct them. The harried circumstances of his life did not allow him to complete the work in definitive form. But he did make interesting and significant changes in the King James Version that can now be traced readily in the new edition of the Bible published by the Church.

To illustrate, in the story of Noah, the King James Bible states that so wicked were men that "it repented the Lord that he had made man on the earth." (Genesis 6:5-6.) The New English Bible states similarly: "He [God] was sorry that he had made man on earth." In the Inspired Version, Joseph Smith wrote: "And it repented Noah . . . that the Lord had made man on the earth." (Genesis 8:13.) It is understandable that the Lord should be discouraged with man's behavior, but it is more reasonable to think, I believe, that Noah should regret the whole human adventure. He had a more limited perspective on man's future than did the Lord.

More significant, perhaps, is a second illustration of Joseph Smith's inspired rendering of a passage of scripture. In the King James Version the Lord appears to Moses and tells him to ask Pharaoh to let his people go. He then says to Moses, "I will harden Pharaoh's heart, and multiply my signs and my wonders in the land of Egypt." (Exodus 7:3.) The New English Bible reads, "I will make him stubborn." It bothered me as a high school freshman, studying the Old Testament, that God would harden Pharaoh's heart in the first place and then punish him and his people for having a hard heart. In the Joseph

Smith Translation we read, "And Pharaoh will harden his heart." This is more consistent with the character of God and the free agency of man.

Another way for Latter-day Saints to check the accuracy of translation is to compare the biblical passage with passages on the same subject in the Book of Mormon or Doctrine and Covenants, whenever they occur. We would expect some consistency among the scriptures, but we must be careful not to infringe on the integrity of the Bible, which should be interpreted and judged essentially on its own merits.

Some Latter-day Saint writers, notably President J. Reuben Clark, Jr., have stressed the preeminence of the King James translation of the Bible. This is natural. It has been used from the beginning of our history to tell the story of the Restoration and to establish the authenticity of our doctrine. For this reason, and because of its unsurpassed literary beauty, deep feelings of reverence are associated with it. Still, the King James translation does have one rather serious drawback for the current reader. It was published in the Elizabethan English of 1611, and many of its words have changed meaning since then. Shakespeare, who wrote his plays in the same period, is difficult to read for the same reason. A simple example or two will illustrate my point. The King James rendition of Matthew 6:25 reads: "Take no thought for your life, what ye shall eat, or what ye shall drink; nor yet for your body, what ye shall put on. Is not the life more than meat . . . ?" A more recent translation reads: "Be not anxious about the morrow. . . ." "Take no thought" in 1611 meant "be not anxious." This makes much more sense than a literal interpretation of "take no thought." In the Joseph Smith Translation, the passage reads in part: "and care not for the world." (See the Joseph Smith Translation in the Latter-day Saint edition of the Bible, p. 802, Matthew 6:25-27.) The Word of Wisdom and our welfare program teach us to take thought.

Some of the modern translations of the Beatitudes also add rich meaning. The first Beatitude in the King

James Bible reads: "Blessed are the poor in spirit." This we have always and quite correctly interpreted as referring to the humble. I like two other renditions equally well: "Blessed are they who feel their spiritual need" and "Blessed are they who feel their dependence on God."

The Church will continue to use the King James Bible as its standard, but we should make judicious use of other translations and Joseph Smith's revision. Some of the more recent translations clear up obscure passages. The New English Bible is particularly helpful in clarifying difficult passages. Martin Luther's translation is revered justifiably by the German people.

We seek correctness of translation so that we can get at the original intent and meaning of the author. To achieve this goal, we must broaden the meaning of translation. I don't know exactly what the word meant to Joseph Smith, but it appears he may have meant "interpreted correctly." His own revision was not a translation but an inspired reinterpretation. The Bible was copied many, many times before the writing of the manuscripts from which extant translations have been made. In the process, errors, additions, or deletions could have been made by devout, well-meaning scribes. The last chapter in the book of Job, for instance, may well have been a later addition. It is so untrue to life that at least in the judgment of many thoughtful students, it really weakens the great message of the book.

To interpret scripture correctly we need to know, if possible, not only the correct translation of the text, but also all the other guides that will be developed in these chapters. We also need to seek the Holy Spirit to guide us—the same Spirit that inspired the writers.

5

The Religious Intent

A friend I knew at college once argued that the Bible couldn't be true because it speaks of the ends of the earth, whereas everyone knows that the earth is a sphere. He was also disturbed by the creation story in Genesis wherein God creates the earth and all things on it in only six days. His geology class did not bear this out.

My friend failed to understand that the Bible is not a scientific text. It is a religious record. References to Mother Nature are there to illustrate a religious purpose, often to glorify God and his power. With rare exceptions they are not made in the spirit of scientific accuracy.[1] This should not surprise us, since modern science did not develop until long after the Bible was written.

In the very beginning of the Genesis story, two great religious concepts are stressed: first, "God created the heaven and the earth," which leaves no doubt that the creation is the work of God; and second, after each act of creation, the scripture states that "God saw that it was good," noting finally that "it was very good." Here are two great ideas: God is the author of creation, and it is meaningful and good because it is his handiwork. Blessed

---

[1]The Word of Wisdom (D&C 89) may be an exception, but even it is religiously oriented, as well as scientifically sound.

is the person of faith who can believe these two things and live life consistent with the will of God that emerges in the rest of the Bible. It is my belief that the author of Genesis had no intention of presenting a scientific analysis of the *how* of creation. He lived in a prescientific age without a scientific vocabulary or interest. But he gloried in God and wanted him to be the foundation and fountain of life. The usage of the word *day* in scripture illustrates the fact that biblical language is not used with scientific intent. In science we give a definite and fixed meaning to a word. It is always used with the same meaning. Authors of scripture have at least four meanings for the word *day:* twenty-four hours (Genesis 1), "as a thousand years" (2 Peter 3:8), a definite period of time (Abraham 4), and an indefinite period of time (Genesis 2:4-5; Alma 40:8;[2] Moses 1:41).

The story of the creation of woman from Adam's rib, if taken as a description of a surgical operation and the origin of Eve's life, raises a lot of questions. If one reads this story looking for religious truth and the wisdom of life, however, it becomes an exciting and wholly believable story. Note the truths it still contains, though told several thousand years ago:

1. It is not good for man to be alone.

2. "Therefore shall a man leave his father and his mother, and shall cleave unto his wife: and they shall be one flesh."

3. "And . . . were not ashamed." (See Genesis 2:18-25.)

I once heard the book of Jonah read to a group of medical students. They squirmed and expressed their disbelief that any creature could survive in a stomach for three days. They were so concerned about the scientific implications of the story that they missed the great religious message of this classic. And what is the religious purpose and meaning of the book of Jonah? You cannot run away from the Lord with impunity is one lesson. But

---

[2]"All is as one day with God, and time only is measured unto men."

this is not the greatest idea in the book. It is that God is universal, a person of justice and mercy. His mercy extends to the people of Nineveh as much as it does to Israel—and on the same conditions. The Israelites of Jonah's day needed to learn that lesson, for they thought they were especially favored by a God who was partial to them. For anyone who has learned the religious truths taught in the book of Jonah, whether or not Jonah was in the fish for three days becomes incidental to the religious teaching and purpose of the book.

The Bible is a profoundly religious book, teaching us of our relationship to God and Christ and of our ethical responsibility to others. References to nature are there to illustrate these important relationships—the very heart of religion.

The Bible is not *anti*-scientific, however. There is a noted absence or a minimum of superstition and irrationality in its pages. The Law of Moses condemns spiritualism, divination, and astrology and encourages obedience to law. The universe was orderly to the Hebrew mind because it was the creation of God. Note this beautiful passage from Proverbs 3:19-26.

> The Lord by wisdom hath founded the earth; by understanding hath he established the heavens. By his knowledge the depths are broken up, and the clouds drop down the dew.
>
> My son, let not them depart from thine eyes: keep sound wisdom and discretion: So shall they be life unto thy soul, and grace to thy neck. Then shalt thou walk in thy way safely, and thy foot shall not stumble. When thou liest down, thou shalt not be afraid: yea, thou shalt lie down, and thy sleep shall be sweet.
>
> Be not afraid of sudden fear, neither of the desolation of the wicked, when it cometh. For the Lord shall be thy confidence, and shall keep thy foot from being taken.

While the author of this passage stresses the wisdom of God in creation, this was not his major purpose. He goes beyond this. He asks us to remember and keep the knowledge and wisdom of God so that we can walk through life unafraid, with confidence, and without stumbling along the way. In other words, his purpose in describing the divine creation is religious.

As the Bible illustrates its religious character on virtually every page, Book of Mormon authors explicitly state again and again their spiritual intent. Nephi writes:

> For the fulness of mine intent is that I may persuade men to come unto . . . God . . . and be saved. (1 Nephi 6:4.)
>
> And I know that the Lord God will consecrate my prayers for the gain of my people. And the words which I have written in weakness will be made strong unto them; for it persuadeth them to do good; it maketh known unto them of their fathers; and it speaketh of Jesus, and persuadeth them to believe in him, and to endure to the end, which is life eternal.
>
> And it speaketh harshly against sin, according to the plainness of the truth; wherefore, no man will be angry at the words which I have written save he shall be of the spirit of the devil. (2 Nephi 33:4-5.)

Nephi's brother Jacob continues the record with the same religious emphasis in Jacob 1:2-8.

The final chapter in the Book of Mormon is an earnest plea to men to come unto Christ and to be perfected in him by his grace. It was Moroni's first and last concern that his people and all who read his record would be persuaded to forsake sin and come unto Christ.

The scriptures are not scientific works in the present meaning of the term, nor are they primarily books of history, philosophy, or even of theology. It is misleading, for instance, to call the Book of Mormon a history of the American Indians. It contains history, but history as a means to an end, instrumental in convincing men that Jesus is the Christ and that they should repent and live as he would have them live. It can be said, then, that the Book of Mormon is a religious record set in a historical framework, but nowhere does it claim to be a history of all peoples in the Americas. There is also much history in the Bible and in the Doctrine and Covenants, but the main purpose of their authors is religious too.

Neither are scriptures theological texts. There is a

difference between theology and religion. Theology is abstract and intellectual, an organized statement of beliefs, of definitions about God and his relationship to man. Religion is living, actual worship of and service to God. The statement in Hebrews (11:1), for instance, that "faith is the substance of things hoped for, the evidence of things not seen" is a theological statement. Likewise, in simpler language, is Alma's definition: ". . . faith is not to have a perfect knowledge of things; therefore if ye have faith ye hope for things which are not seen, which are true." (Alma 32:21.) These are two of the few statements in the scriptures about faith that might be called theological. There are, on the other hand, hundreds of illustrations of men and women living by faith—demonstrations of religion. There are theological concepts in scripture, but they are found in a larger setting of religious experience.

Scriptures should be read and interpreted in the same spirit and with the same emphasis with which they were written. Anyone who does not recognize the essential religious character of scripture will miss the mark and misjudge these rich and unusual writings. Anyone who will look for religious teachings and inspiration in the scriptures will find them in great abundance.

6

Inspired of God but in Man's Language

Elder John A. Widtsoe had an interesting point of view on scripture: "The message of the scripture is divine; the words in which it is clothed are human. Failure to make this distinction has led to much misunderstanding. Intelligent readers will separate the message of the scripture from its form of presentation." (*The Articles of Faith in Everyday Life* [YM and YWMIA of The Church of Jesus Christ of Latter-day Saints, 1949], p. 60.)

This same idea is stated in scripture itself: "For my soul delighteth in plainness; for after this manner doth the Lord God work among the children of men. For the Lord God giveth light unto the understanding; for he speaketh unto men according to *their* language, unto *their* understanding." (2 Nephi 31:3. Italics added.)

As one reads scripture, one must think not only of God and his purposes, but also of men, of the writer, and of his audience, and not expect perfection. Brigham Young implies this in his forthright style:

> I am so far from believing that any government upon this earth has constitutions and laws that are perfect, that I do not even believe there is a single revelation, among the many God has given to the Church, that is perfect in its fulness. The revelations of God contain correct doctrines and principle, as far as they go; but it is impossible for the poor, weak, low,

grovelling, sinful inhabitants of the earth to receive a revelation from the Almighty in all its perfections. He has to speak to us in a manner to meet the extent of our capacities. (*Journal of Discourses* 2:314.)

Man plays a most significant role in both translating and creating scripture. The Lord's instruction to Oliver Cowdery explaining why he failed in his attempt to translate the Book of Mormon applies also to the receiving and writing of revelation.

Behold, you have not understood; you have supposed that I would give it unto you, when you took no thought save it was to ask me.

But, behold, I say unto you, that you must study it out in your mind; then you must ask me if it be right, and if it is right I will cause that your bosom shall burn within you; therefore, you shall feel that it is right.

But if it be not right you shall have no such feelings, but you shall have a stupor of thought that shall cause you to forget the thing which is wrong; therefore, you cannot write that which is sacred save it be given you from me.

Now, if you had known this you could have translated; nevertheless, it is not expedient that you should translate now. (D&C 9:7-10.)

My favorite passage in all of scripture on the nature of revelation is found in the Doctrine and Covenants. It applies equally to scripture because much of it is a record of revelation.

Behold, I am God and have spoken it; these commandments are of me, and were given unto my servants in their weakness, after the manner of their language, that they might come to understanding.

And inasmuch as they erred it might be made known;

And inasmuch as they sought wisdom they might be instructed;

And inasmuch as they sinned they might be chastened, that they might repent;

And inasmuch as they were humble they might be made

strong, and blessed from on high, and receive knowledge from time to time. (D&C 1:24-28.)

Revelation is of God and it is authoritative for the believer, but it is given in man's language and weakness, in his own thinking and understanding. Much of it is correction of sin and error or affirmation of correct thinking—but always in words man understands. Men do violence to scripture if they ascribe every word of it to God.

Various books of scripture reflect the character and style of their respective authors: Paul's eloquent descriptions of the saving grace of Jesus Christ, John's great emphasis on love, and James's down-to-earth practical religion are all inspired, but each is unique in language and content. In studying the scriptures we should appreciate the contributions of both Deity and human writers.

There is much in scripture that is so beautiful, powerful, and rich in meaning that one can believe it is wholly of God. Examples are the Ten Commandments, the Beatitudes, Paul's eulogy on love (1 Corinthians 13), the twenty-third psalm, Doctrine and Covenants 121, and Micah 6:6-8. The authors certainly rise above their own capability under inspiration of Deity in these and many other passages. But they use the words of men and they reflect their own feeling as well as divine inspiration. The words of Micah illustrate the heights prophetic utterance reaches:

> Wherewith shall I come before the Lord, and bow myself before the high God? shall I come before him with burnt offerings, with calves of a year old?
> Will the Lord be pleased with thousands of rams, or with ten thousands of rivers of oil? shall I give my firstborn for my transgression, the fruit of my body for the sin of my soul?
> He hath showed thee, O man, what is good; and what doth the Lord require of thee, but to do justly, and to love mercy, and to walk humbly with thy God? (Micah 6:6-8.)

Other passages of scripture reflect the author's viewpoint or are conditioned markedly by the circumstances and comprehension of his audience. This is true particularly of some of the narrative and historical portions of the Old Testament, which are not always on the same high plane that characterizes the writings of the prophets. For example, 2 Kings 2:23-24 tells the story of Elisha as he was mocked by little children who said to him, "Go up, thou bald head." It says that when he cursed them in the name of the Lord, two "she bears" came out of the woods and attacked forty-two children, supposedly killing them. This implies divine retribution for their lack of respect for a prophet. I, however, am unable to imagine Jehovah, Jesus Christ in the meridian of time, the same Jesus Christ who loved little children, turning bears upon them in their innocent folly. In my judgment the author meant to show respect for the prophet Elisha, but lacked understanding of the character of God in ascribing such action to him.

The commandments in the law of Moses are, for the most part, just and humane and superior to the ethical standards of surrounding tribes and nations. Much of the law is on as high a plane as the teachings of Jesus. This is illustrated in the holiness code found in Leviticus, chapters 19-26. The Israelites were told not to reap the corners of their fields nor to glean their vineyards and grain fields, but to leave them for the poor and the stranger. (Leviticus 19:9-10.) This is also illustrated in the beautiful story of Ruth. Israelites were taught to be no respecters of persons but to respect the poor as much as the mighty and to love the stranger as one born among them. On the other hand, there are practices in the law of Moses that are related to the times and that we would consider unethical today. Hebrews as well as Gentiles were sold into slavery in ancient Israel, but within this practice, slave owners were admonished to release slaves after a given period of time and to send them away with a stock of goods from their master's storehouse.

Under the law of Moses there was no tolerance of the dissenter from Israel's faith. Anyone professing other gods and encouraging others to do so was to be stoned without pity. This is a far cry from our eleventh Article of Faith, which allows all men to worship what they will. It is understandable only if we remember that Israelites lived among peoples steeped in idolatry and that Israelites were sorely tempted to imitate their neighbors. (See Deuteronomy 13.)

According to the law of Moses, a rebellious son who refused to change his ways was to be brought before the elders and stoned to death. (Deuteronomy 21:18-21.) In this way serious problems in family life would be done away with in Israel. Despite all the problems faced between parents and children today, I am glad that we are no longer commanded to kill sons who are beyond control.

The law of Moses is a complex, fascinating combination of just, considerate, and humane laws sprinkled here and there with laws that seem unduly harsh and even unjust. The only explanation I know for the limitations of this great effort to establish a righteous society in Israel is to ascribe them to men. In some instances, God may have accepted and condoned a lower law to meet human need, as he did in letting Israel have a king. In other instances, I believe writers of Israel's history gave credit or blame to God for actions and decrees that were unworthy of him under any circumstances.

7

Reading in Context

Shakespeare's remark in the preface to this book is worth repeating:

In religion,
What damned error, but some sober brow
Will bless it, and approve it with a text
Hiding the grossness with fair ornament?
　　—Merchant of Venice, *act 3, sc. 2*

Over the centuries men in various churches and sects have quoted single verses or passages of the Bible to prove their particular beliefs. Sometimes these texts are used correctly; at other times they do violence to the author's meaning. Using a passage of scripture isolated from its larger setting is called text-proof method. It is often unfair.

A colleague of mine was asked to review a book of which he was extremely and justifiably critical. It lacked historical accuracy, logic, and substance. He did say in one sentence that it was well-written. The publishers then latched on to that one favorable comment. Ignoring his total review, they quoted it as propaganda to promote the sale of the book, a nonscriptural illustration of quoting out of context and dishonesty.

Context means *with the text*. There are three kinds of context: (1) the immediate setting of a passage, (2) its place in the book of which the passage is a part, such as Amos, Job, or Galatians, and (3) its relationship to the gospel as a whole, especially the fundamentals.

In the Context of the Passage

It is perfectly proper to quote a single verse or two of scripture, but in doing so one should have read what precedes it and what follows it. Otherwise he may misrepresent the author's idea. The following story illustrates this.

One evening in a city in Switzerland a Mormon missionary gave a talk to non-Mormons on the nature of God. He endeavored to demonstrate that the Father was a real person—a Creator, Revelator, and Father in whose image man was made. Suddenly a minister in the back of the hall cried out, "God is a Spirit," quoting from John 4:24. In this verse, Jesus was not trying to describe the whole nature of God; he was emphasizing the role of spirit in God and man as part of a brief discourse on how to worship. He was trying to teach the Samaritan woman to worship "in spirit and in truth."

In that same meeting a few moments later, the minister spoke up again, saying, "God is love," quoting correctly from 1 John 4:8. He was using the verse to prove that God is love and nothing else. If we turn to this verse, however, and read the verses before and after that complete the thought (verses 7-12), we see again that the main interest was to inspire people to love one another. To achieve this, the author stressed God's great attribute of love. The Father's love for us is so great that he is the embodiment of love; this is one of his greatest attributes. But he is also more than love. The next verse says: "In this was manifested the love of God toward us, because that God sent his only begotten Son into the world, that we might live through him." (1 John 4:9.) Love alone cannot send us a savior, cannot create worlds, cannot bring to pass the resurrection. Love is a quality that cannot exist except as a single attribute. It lives through those who exercise it.

In their missionary zeal, Latter-day Saints are sometimes guilty of quoting verses out of context. Isaiah 4:1 speaks of the day when seven women shall take hold of one man and ask to be called by his name. In the past, it was common for missionaries to defend the practice of plural marriage with this verse, which to them was a prophecy of the practice of plural marriage. We might well gather this notion by reading this verse alone. If, however, we begin reading in chapter 3, from verse 16 to the end, we readily see that 4:1 belongs to the same train of thought as Isaiah 3:16-26. Isaiah sees that war is coming to Judah, and that the proud women of Judea, who are more concerned with decorating their faces and bodies than they are with the affliction of the poor in Israel, have made their contribution to the downfall of the nation. Not only have they lived in vain and idle luxury, but they have encouraged their masters to cheat and lie to get gain, living lives offensive to God and destructive of national unity and strength. What happens to women in time of war? Their men fall in battle and they become widows. Marriage meant much to the women of Israel; hence, in the day of calamity (which was near at hand) there might be seven women to one man. Isaiah was depicting the consequences of war brought on by unrighteousness. His prediction applies widely in human experience and is not a prediction of plural marriage.

In the Context of the Book

Each of the standard works is a collection of many writings or books. The Old Testament has thirty-nine, the New Testament twenty-seven, for example. Each passage of scripture is part of a writing or book within one of the standard works. It should be interpreted as part of that writing or book.

Part of one verse in the beautiful twenty-third psalm reads: "Thou anointest my head with oil." In a Sunday School class one day a teacher used this statement to prove that the anointing of the sick was practiced in the Old Testament. It may have been, but this was not the verse to use to prove it. The entire twenty-third psalm is a song of thanksgiving and praise to the Lord. "Thou anointest my head with oil" is a symbolic way of acknowledging the bounteous blessings and goodness of the Lord—as the entire psalm attests. If you wish to prove that the anointing of the sick was used in biblical times, turn to the book of James, a work of forthright admonition and instruction, and there you will find this explicit teaching: "Is any sick among you? let him call for the elders of the church; and let them pray over him, anointing him with oil in the name of the Lord: And the prayer of faith shall save the sick, and the Lord shall raise him up; and if he have committed sins, they shall be forgiven him." (James 5:14-15.)

In Ezekiel 37, a vision of this prophet is recorded wherein he saw a valley full of dry bones and then saw flesh and sinews come upon them, "Breath came into them, and they lived." (Ezekiel 37:10.) Verses 1-14 of this passage have been used to prove the resurrection. It is probably not Ezekiel's purpose in this passage to establish the doctrine of individual resurrection. It is quite obvious, if one reads the entire book of Ezekiel, that the prophet is talking about the restoration of Israel as a nation, as a people, with dry bones as a symbol of their captivity. The resurrection can be established much more clearly and abundantly in the New Testament or Book of Mormon. (Note Alma 40, Luke 24, and 1 Corinthians 15.)

Latter-day Saints should also read the rest of chapter 37 with Ezekiel's purpose in mind. Verses 15-28 tell the oft-repeated account of the prophet being commanded to write upon two sticks, one for Judah and one for Joseph,

Judah being interpreted as the Bible and Joseph as the Book of Mormon. If we read the entire passage in the context of the total book of Ezekiel, we will find that the prophet is predicting not only the coming forth of two books or records, but also the restoration and reunion of the two nations—Israel and Judah. The Bible and Book of Mormon are records of Judah and Joseph, respectively, and the coming forth of these two records heralds the eventual reunion of the two nations and should some day even contribute to Israel's unification. The coming forth of the Book of Mormon fits into this larger hope and faith of the prophet Ezekiel. Latter-day Saints often ignore Ezekiel's great interest in unifying Israel and Judah.

To see how a great passage of scripture assumes even more meaning when read as part of an entire writing, refer to 1 Corinthians, one of Paul's most interesting epistles. Paul had learned that there were contentions among the Saints (1:10) and all manner of strife, divisions, and sins (3:1-3). Some of their strife was over the gifts of the gospel. Some could speak in tongues, some could not; some could interpret, others could not. In chapter 12 Paul explains the gifts of the gospel and how different gifts are enjoyed by different members but not all by all. In chapter 14 he explains that the gift of tongues is not the most important gift of the gospel nor is it a necessary one. Then, in the most meaningful eulogy of brotherly love ever written in scripture, Paul points out the supremacy of love over all other gifts. Without charity (meaning brotherly love and, in Moroni's words, "the pure love of Christ") we are nothing.

> Though I speak with the tongues of men and of angels, and have not charity, I am become as sounding brass, or a tinkling cymbal.
> And though I have the gift of prophecy, and understand all mysteries, and all knowledge; and though I have all faith, so that I could remove mountains, and have not charity, I am nothing.
> And though I bestow all my goods to feed the poor, and though I give my body to be burned and have not charity, it profiteth me nothing. (1 Corinthians 13:1-3.)

Chapter 13 can stand alone, but knowing chapters 12 and 14 adds rich meaning to it.

In the Context of the Gospel

A young architect once gave a group of students and me a choice insight into how to interpret scripture. He was talking about architecture, a highly complex field that embraces art, science, and mathematics. He said architects use three basic guides when planning a garage, house, or a cathedral: Is it sound? Is it functional? Is it beautiful or aesthetically pleasing? These wonderful guidelines are equally useful to the client who is building or buying a home.

Religion too is a vast, complex field. The scriptures, our best record of religion, are tremendously composite, varied in style and origin, written by scores of authors living over centuries. To interpret scripture fairly, intelligently, and meaningfully, we need some guidelines comparable to those of the architect. There is a logical, meaningful, conceptual structure to the gospel just as there is to architecture or any other discipline. Gospel principles belong together; they support and enrich one another. The gospel may be likened to a mosaic. It has a design, a set of ideas that are consistent with each other and that together give meaning to life. The person who would understand religion should not pulverize the gospel and think of it as an array of separate facts and ideas. Like architecture, the gospel has its fundamental concepts and principles. These need to be kept in mind as we read single verses or contemplate individual ideas in scripture. To illustrate, I suggest that there are some fundamental concepts regarding God and man that should always be remembered as we read the scriptures.

Our conception of God the Father:
1. He is the Father of all men.
2. He has certain moral attributes, such as justice, impartiality, integrity, love, mercy, forgiveness.

3. He is law-abiding.

4. He is more intelligent than all other persons.

Our conception of man:

1. All men are children of God.

2. All men are brothers.

3. Men are that they might have joy.

4. Men have the capacity through obedience to the principles of the gospel to progress eternally.

5. Men have free agency.

6. Men were created in the image of God.

These concepts concerning God and man represent only a partial listing to illustrate the value of interpreting scripture in the light of fundamentals.

A Case Study

In Alma 34, which is a profound and rich chapter, we read:

> And now, as I said unto you before, as ye have had so many witnesses, therefore, I beseech of you, that ye do not procrastinate the day of your repentance until the end; for after this day of life, which is given us to prepare for eternity, behold, if we do not improve our time while in this life, then cometh the night of darkness wherein there can be no labor performed.
>
> Ye cannot say, when ye are brought to that awful crisis, that I will repent, that I will return to my God. Nay, ye cannot say this; for that same spirit which doth possess your bodies at the time that ye go out of this life, that same spirit will have power to possess your body in that eternal world.
>
> For behold, if ye have procrastinated the day of your repentance, even until death, behold, ye have become subjected to the spirit of the devil, and he doth seal you his; therefore, the Spirit of the Lord hath withdrawn from you, and hath no place in you, and the devil hath all power over you; and this is the final state of the wicked. (Alma 34:33-35.)

How do we interpret this passage? Is there no opportunity whatever for repentance in life beyond the grave? Some people think so, and that may be right with regard to those who are spiritually dead. Taking this passage by itself, with no reference to other gospel fundamentals, we could easily conclude this. But let us remember that God is our Father—a loving, merciful Father—and that his work and glory is to redeem his children. He is not likely to give up easily nor quickly. Judging by the attitude of his Son, the Father would, we believe, never close the door to repentance for his children.

Some, such as the sons of perdition, may sink so low that they lose the power to repent because they "die as to things pertaining unto righteousness." (Alma 12:16.) Perhaps others who have procrastinated their repentance may find the faith and power to repent in the eternal world. This is our faith when we do work for our kindred dead, some of whom, no doubt, were first-rate sinners. We are not discrediting Amulek's plea to repent now. It is the sensible thing to do, for happiness in this life as well as for our eternal welfare. And no one knows who will have the strength to repent hereafter.

The whole gospel cannot be taught in one sermon. However, as we interpret a sermon we can and should do so in the context of the gospel as a whole.

I learned long ago that single verses must be interpreted in the context of the gospel as a whole. A returned missionary said to me that he was in a hurry to get married in the temple because if he were—even though he might commit any sin except murder and the shedding of innocent blood—he would still enter into his exaltation. He based his faith on Doctrine and Covenants 132:26, which says:

> Verily, verily, I say unto you, if a man marry a wife according to my word, and they are sealed by the Holy Spirit of promise, according to mine appointment, and he or she shall commit any sin or transgression of the new and everlasting covenant whatever, and all manner of blasphemies, and if they commit no murder wherein they shed innocent blood, yet they shall come forth in the first resurrection, and enter into their exaltation; but they shall be destroyed in the flesh, and shall be delivered unto the buffetings of Satan unto the day of redemption, saith the Lord God.

33

We might agree with him if we consider this verse in a vacuum. But in the light of the gospel, no unclean thing will enter the presence of God. And no forgiveness is possible without repentance. No verse of scripture intends to give license to sin.

I do not accept any interpretation of scripture that denies the impartiality or love of God or the free agency and brotherhood of man. These concepts are too basic to the gospel to be denied by someone's interpretation of a verse of scripture.

No part of the gospel stands alone, any more than a part of a house does. And just as each part of a house derives its meaning and function in its relationship to the whole house, so it is in the gospel. Single gospel ideas must be viewed as part of a whole plan or perspective. We should try to see the gospel as a whole, not as a series of isolated concepts.

8

Standards of Evaluation

How do we decide which teachings in scripture are valid for us today? How do we distinguish between that which is universally and eternally valid and that which was meant for a particular time and place and which may not be applicable now? How do we determine that which is of God and that which may have crept into scripture through the errors or misinterpretations of well-meaning writers, scribes, or translators?

To answer these questions, we should employ all the guidelines thus far discussed in this work—the background, authorship, correctness of translation, context, and religious intent. But these are not enough. To avoid error or justifying our own desires we need additional rational and spiritual helps. What are some of these?

Consistent with Gospel Fundamentals

If we study all scriptures, certain fundamentals emerge clearly. One is the character of God. Over and over again in all four scriptures Jesus and the prophets bear witness that God is our Father—just, impartial, merciful, forgiving, law-abiding, creative, and intelligent. If we believe the scriptures, we can depend on God's integrity and love.

Isolated passages may portray him as wrathful or jealous or capricious, but these attributes do not square with the above-named qualities of character. Therefore, passages that appear to portray him so negatively must be reviewed and interpreted carefully to preserve the integrity and consistency of his character. For example, the word *jealous*, as we use it, usually describes weakness in human character, based on a feeling of inadequacy and insecurity, and often nurturing envy and hate. Surely God is not of such a character. Actually, the word *jealous* in its scriptural usage may mean *one cares.* Webster gives an archaic meaning of jealousy as "earnest concern or solicitude; vigilant watchfulness or care." In the new Latter-day Saint edition of the Bible, the word *jealous* taken from the Hebrew "qannah" is interpreted as "possessing sensitive and deep feelings." (See Genesis 20:5, footnote b.) This makes sense. Likewise in human experience a person who knows wrath is usually out of his mind, beyond self-control. Our Father must experience righteous indignation as did Jesus when he drove money changers from the temple courtyard. Yet the Savior was always in control of himself.

I do not accept any interpretation of scriptural passages that portrays God as being partial, unforgiving, hateful, or revengeful. It is more important to uphold the character and will of God than it is to support every line of scripture.

Clearly portrayed in the scriptures are certain concepts of the nature of man. Taken as a whole they repeatedly teach or imply free agency, the brotherhood of man, God's concern for man, man's responsibility for his own behavior, and certain basic ethical requirements such as those that we find in the Decalogue. Certain isolated passages, if taken singly, may seem to deny some of these principles. For instance, in Ephesians Paul states, "For by grace are ye saved through faith; and that not of yourselves: it is the gift of God: Not of works, lest any man should boast." (Ephesians 2:8-9.) This passage seems to imply that salvation is wholly an act of grace.

This kind of interpretation and logic may have led John Calvin, the great French Protestant reformer, to teach predestination. Many Protestant groups rely wholly on the grace of Christ. If we study all scriptures, including Ezekiel, James, the Book of Mormon, and Doctrine and Covenants—and even Paul's writings—we will find that the grace of Christ plays a large role in our lives. But to make it efficacious in relation to our sins, we must also exercise faith unto repentance. To maintain that man has no role in his own salvation besides simple acceptance of Christ is to make his free agency, repentance, and personal spiritual growth quite meaningless. I believe the scriptures strike a happy balance between the grace of Deity and the faith and works of the individual, both being essential to life and eternal salvation.

Consistent with Christ's Spirit and Teachings

Since Christ is the Son of God and unexcelled in his own character, mind, and close relationship to the Father, since he inherited all the rich background of the law and the prophets, and since we profess to be his disciples, he should be our ultimate standard as we interpret and use scriptures in our own lives.

If any concepts, attitudes, and practices of the Israelites, Nephites, Lamanites, or Latter-day Saints contradict the Savior's teachings, we should study them further. First, we must be sure our interpretation is not at fault; then we should not accept and practice principles and policies that are contrary to Christ's spirit and example. Brigham Young stated this thought very well: "We have taken this book, called the Old and the New Testament for our standard. We believe this book and receive it as the word of the Lord. Not but there are many words in this book that are not the words of the Lord, but, that which came from the heavens, and which the Lord has delivered to us, we receive, and especially the sayings of the Savior." (*Journal of Discourses* 12:309.)

Continuous Revelation

Since men are not infallible, and since life is dynamic and characterized by change, continuous revelation is needed to correct errors of the past and to implement the basic, eternal principles of the gospel into the policies and practices of both individuals and the Church today. We need prophets—men called and inspired of God—to interpret the meaning of the gospel for our time.

Needed also in the Church's and our personal interpretation of scripture is the gift of discernment through the Holy Ghost and the light of Christ. The truths of scripture were inspired of the Holy Spirit. Therefore, their interpretation should be guided by the same spirit that produced them.

Common Sense

A fine German brother and former mission president said to me one day as he helped me build a room in our house, "I go to Sunday School and listen to all kinds of gospel interpretations. I have decided not to believe anything that doesn't make good 'horses senses.' "

I remember a college girl in Sunday School who quoted an interpretation by her teacher of religion. Her idea didn't make sense to the class or to me, so I asked her what she meant. She replied, "I don't know what it means either, but Brother _____ taught it to me, and I believe it."

Faith takes us beyond knowledge, but I don't see how any interpretation of scripture can be enlightening if we don't understand it. I think too that we should question interpretations that contradict common sense, good judgment, verified experience, and the counsel of wise and good men and women. I believe reason should confirm what we believe to be the inspiration of the Holy Ghost, and I believe we also should check our own thinking by the Holy Spirit.

Oliver Cowdery, in his failure to translate the Book

of Mormon, learned the necessity of combining thinking with divine inspiration in the work of the Lord. (See D&C 9:7-10.) I believe the counsel given to him applies to the interpretation of scripture as well as to its translation.

In Christ's great summary of the religious life he said, repeating an ancient law, "Thou shalt love the Lord thy God with all thy *heart,* and with all thy soul, and with all thy *mind.*" (Matthew 22:37. Italics added.)

An interpretation of scripture can be trusted when it (1) is consistent with gospel fundamentals and with the teachings and spirit of Christ, (2) is confirmed by the promptings of the Spirit, (3) appeals to our ethical judgment, and (4) has won agreement among persons of good will. Of such a nature as this is the memorable revelation received by President Spencer W. Kimball on June 8, 1978, in which the priesthood was made available to all worthy male members of the Church regardless of race. This revelation is wholly consistent with the impartiality of God, the love of Christ, and the free agency of man. It appeals to our ethical judgment, has been received by men and women of good will, and has been confirmed by the Holy Spirit in the minds and hearts of Church leaders and members overwhelmingly. It has been accepted by the Church and has become part of our modern scripture, the Doctrine and Covenants.

9

Scripture as Literature

Literature worthy of the name must have two qualities—significant substance and beautiful, expressive language. Judged by these criteria, the scriptures contain much that is good, even great, literature. Their greatness is the consequence of deep feeling and conviction and inspired utterance about things that really matter—life and death, right and wrong, and the meaning of human existence, as well as by the ability to express thoughts effectively and beautifully.

Among the standard works, the Bible stands preeminent as literature. And within the Bible, the Old Testament has more great literature than any other scripture. The Old Testament is three times as large as the New Testament and also richer in its variety of literary expression because it contains narration, history, epics, wisdom literature, oratory, proverbs, hymns, stories, and a dramatic debate. Teachers of Bible literature spend most of their time on the Old Testament. The New Testament, however, is also rich in literary quality, and the other scriptures also boast fine literary passages.

As much as we read the scriptures to learn the will of the Lord in doctrine and conduct and to study history, Church organization, and policy, we can and should also read them for sheer enjoyment, for the aesthetic response that they bring forth in us. Aesthetic feeling in itself, one of the rich, spiritual experiences of life, creates a sense of wholeness and peace. Reading the scriptures with an appreciation of their beauty of expression is akin to worship. Psalm 23 and Isaiah 40-66, from which some of the themes of Handel's *Messiah* were taken, illustrate how scriptures inspire worship.

The Bible as Literature

One of the distinctive features of Hebrew writing is called parallelism, synonymous parallelism being its most common form. Many Hebrew writers could not say something once and be done with it. They loved to repeat the same thought in slightly different form, twice or as many as seven times. This literary form gives the reader opportunity to contemplate the author's meaning, to let it sink into mind and heart. Note the following parallel verses from the first chapter of Isaiah:

The ox knoweth his owner,
and the ass his master's crib;
but Israel doth not know,
my people doth not consider. (Verse 3.)

Your country is desolate,
your cities are burned with fire:
your land, strangers devour it in your presence,
and it is desolate, as overthrown by strangers. (Verse 7.)

Ah sinful nation,
a people laden with iniquity,
a seed of evil doers,
children that are corrupters:
they have forsaken the Lord,
they have provoked the Holy One of Israel unto anger,
they are gone away backward. (Verse 4.)

Wash you,
make you clean;

put away the evil of your doings . . .
cease to do evil. (Verse 16.)

Learn to do well;
seek judgment [justice],
relieve the oppressed,
judge the fatherless,
plead for the widow. (Verse 17.)

Other features of biblical writing are its simplicity and concreteness and its wide use of nouns and verbs with minimal presence of adjectives and adverbs. Biblical stories, parables, and exhortations by the prophets waste no words, produce vivid pictures, and kindle the imagination. Genesis, for example, is essentially a book of narration rich in human interest, telling of the lives of Cain and Abel, Noah, Abraham, Isaac and Rebekah, Jacob and Leah, Rachel and Esau, and Joseph. Note how much is told in the two short verses that introduce the Joseph epic:

"Now Israel loved Joseph more than all his children, because he was the son of his old age: and he made him a coat of many colours. And when his brethren saw that their father loved him more than all his brethren, they hated him, and could not speak peaceably unto him." (Genesis 37:3-4.)

Near the end of the Joseph story, Joseph insists that his brothers—who do not recognize him—bring his younger, full brother, Benjamin, to Egypt if they wish to obtain any grain. They finally do bring Benjamin. Joseph has a silver cup placed in Benjamin's sack so that he can be brought back, ostensibly for stealing. Judah's plea to let Benjamin return to their aged father is moving: "Now therefore, I pray thee, let thy servant abide instead of the lad a bondman to my lord; and let the lad go up with his brethren. For how shall I go up to my father, and the lad be not with me? lest peradventure I see the evil that shall come on my father." (Genesis 44:33-34.) This concern and magnanimity on the part of Judah was too much for

Joseph, who wept aloud and made himself known to his brethren.

The Joseph story is beautifully told, full of conflict and suspense. It reveals not only an ideal character in Joseph, but one that personifies much of the best in Israel as a nation.

The Bible is rich in figures of speech, in abundance of metaphors and similes. Listen to Amos: "Hear this word, ye kine of Bashan, that are in the mountain of Samaria, which oppress the poor, which crush the needy, which say to their masters, Bring, and let us drink." (Amos 4:1.) The kine (cattle) of Bashan, a rich pasture land of Israel, are the rich women of Israel who encourage their husbands to provide a luxurious life for them at the expense of the poor, if need be.

Note the similes in Hosea:

> O Ephraim, what shall I do unto thee? O Judah, what shall I do unto thee? for your goodness is as a morning cloud, and as the early dew it goeth away. (Hosea 6:4.)
> Ephraim also is like a silly dove without heart: they call to Egypt, they go to Assyria. When they shall go, I will spread my net upon them; I will bring them down as the fowls of the heaven. . . . (Hosea 7:11-12.)

Job's lament over the tragedy of human life is beautiful pathos:

> Man that is born of a woman is of few days, and full of trouble.
> He cometh forth like a flower, and is cut down: he fleeth also as a shadow, and continueth not. . . .
> For there is hope of a tree, if it be cut down, that it will sprout again, and that the tender branch thereof will not cease.
> Though the root thereof wax old in the earth, and the stock thereof die in the ground;
> Yet through the scent of water it will bud, and bring forth boughs like a plant.
> But man dieth, and wasteth away: Yea, man giveth up the ghost, and where is he? (Job 14:1-2, 7-10.)

Jesus' words are rich in figurative language, through which he taught memorable truths. To illustrate, "Ye are the salt of the earth" and "Ye are the light of the world." (Matthew 5:13-14.)

Jesus likened the kingdom of God to "a grain of mustard seed, which a man took, and cast into his garden; and it grew, and waxed a great tree; and the fowls of the air lodged in the branches of it." (Luke 13:9.)

And again, the kingdom of God "is like leaven, which a woman took and hid in three measures of meal, till the whole was leavened." (Luke 13:21.)

The whole Bible is interspersed with vivid expressions similar to those above. The following writings of the Old Testament particularly are of great literary merit:

The Law	*The Prophets*	*The Writings*
Genesis	Amos	Psalms
Deuteronomy	Hosea	Job
	Micah	Ecclesiastes
	Isaiah	Ruth
	Jeremiah	
	Jonah	

The above-named prophets have astounding depth expressed in powerful and poetic form. They are often difficult to understand without a Bible commentary or an informed teacher.

The New Testament

The New Testament was written originally in Greek, with perhaps some Aramaic in the Gospels. According to Goodspeed, a great Greek scholar who has translated the Greek New Testament into English, the original language was quite ordinary, everyday Greek. In fact, Goodspeed's translation of the New Testament puts the language into ordinary English. The forty-seven English scholars who published the King James authorized version of the Bible in 1611 improved on the original Greek. They translated it into elegant English. Their entire Bible is truly a work of art that can be read throughout for its literary beauty as well as inspirational truths. Their translation of the Bible drew much from Tyndale's fine work of the previous century.

The New Testament contains great literature in the words of Jesus, the eloquence of Paul, the vigor of James, and the spirit of love in the epistles of John. Read, for example, the parables of the good Samaritan and the prodigal son in Luke 10 and 15; the Sermon on the Mount in Matthew 5, 6, and 7; Paul's eulogy on love in 1 Corinthians 13; John's writings on love in 1 John; Peter's writings on Christian virtues in 2 Peter 1:1-8; and James's discussion of practical religion in the book of James.

The Book of Mormon

Book of Mormon authors make no claim to literary greatness. The first and last of them, Nephi and Moroni, acknowledge their limitations and ask readers not to let their weakness in writing turn them away from the worth of their message. Nephi says, "Now I, Nephi, . . . [am not] mighty in writing, like unto speaking." (2 Nephi 33:1.) And Moroni writes: "Condemn me not because of mine imperfection, neither my father, because of his imperfection, neither them who have written before him; but rather give thanks unto God that he hath made manifest unto you our imperfections, that ye may learn to be more wise than we have been." (Mormon 9:31.)

Notwithstanding these acknowledged limitations by Nephi and Moroni, the Book of Mormon stirs the sincere reader not only through the content of its message, but also with the quality of its writing. Its literary character was probably enriched, like much of the Bible, by its authors' deep religious convictions. The following are illustrations of fine writing from the Book of Mormon and references to other passages that can be read with profit for sheer enjoyment.

After the death of father Lehi, the full burden of leading the major Book of Mormon colony fell upon the shoulders of Nephi. The tragedy of that burden was the hatred he had experienced from his older brothers, Laman and Lemuel, and a foreboding of the evil that lay ahead. In his moment of despair he uttered a psalmlike prayer to God. (Read 2 Nephi 4:15-35. I quote verses 28-30.)

Awake, my soul!
  No longer droop in sin.
Rejoice, O my heart,
  and give place no more
  for the enemy of my soul.
Do not anger again because of mine enemies.
Do not slacken my strength
  because of my afflictions.

Rejoice, O my heart,
  and cry unto the Lord, and say:
  O Lord, I will praise thee forever;
  yea, my soul will rejoice in thee,
  my God, and the rock of my salvation.

The Book of Mormon, like the Bible, has considerable synonymous parallelism, indicative of Hebrew influence, which also adds beauty and interest to its style. Note, for example, 2 Nephi 9:50-52:

Come, my brethren,
  every one that thirsteth,
  come ye to the waters;
and he that hath no money,
  come buy and eat;
  yea, come buy wine and milk
  without money and without price.

Wherefore, do not spend money
  for that which is of no worth,
  nor your labor
  for that which cannot satisfy.
Hearken diligently unto me,
and remember the words which I have spoken;
and come unto the Holy One of Israel,
  and feast upon that which perisheth not,
  neither can be corrupted,
and let your soul delight in fatness.

Behold, my beloved brethren,
  remember the words of your God;
  pray unto him continually by day,
  and give thanks unto his holy name by night.
Let your hearts rejoice.

Note the parallelism in this strategem described in Alma
55:13:

And it came to pass . . .
  they did take of the wine freely;
  and it was pleasant to their taste,
  therefore they took of it more freely;
and it was strong,
having been prepared in its strength.
(Alma 55:13. Read also verses 8-14.)

Helaman despairs at one point with the frailty of
human goodness. Parallelism is also present in this passage, Helaman 12:4-8:

O how foolish,
  and how vain,
  and how evil,

and devilish
and how quick to do iniquity,
and how slow to do good,
Are the children of men;

Yea, *how quick to hearken*
unto the words of the evil one,
and to set their hearts
upon the vain things of the world!
Yea, *how quick to be lifted up in pride;*
yea, how quick to boast,
and do all manner of that which is iniquity,
and how slow are they to remember
the Lord their God,
and to give ear unto his counsels,
yea, how slow to walk in wisdom's paths!

Behold, *they do not desire*
that the Lord their God,
who created them,
should rule and reign over them;
Notwithstanding *his great goodness*
and his mercy towards them,
they do set at naught his counsels,
and they will not that he
should be their guide.

O *how great is the nothingness*
of the children of men;
Yea, *even they are less than*
the dust of the earth.
For behold, *the dust of the earth*
moveth hither and thither,
to the dividing asunder,
At *the command of our great*
and everlasting God.

The reader will find in the Book of Mormon simple

but profound ideas couched in lucid language. Contemplate for example, Mosiah 18, on baptism; Moroni 4 and 5, the sacramental prayers; Alma 32, on faith, its growth and its fruits; Alma 7, a plea to repent; and Moroni 8:24-26, the results of repentance.

The Doctrine and Covenants

This latter-day scripture is rich in content, contributing substantially to our understanding of Church doctrine, organization, functions, priesthood, and ordinances, and the will of God in our everyday living both as individuals and as a people. It is not only important reading on the basis of content, but it also has many beautiful passages that should be read for enjoyment and inspiration because of their literary quality. The revelations combine richness of thought with simplicity and clarity of expression. Note the following passages as illustration:

On the nature of revelation:
Behold, I am God and have spoken it; these commandments are of me, and were given unto my servants in their weakness, after the manner of their language, that they might come to understanding.

And inasmuch as they erred it might be made known; And inasmuch as they sought wisdom they might be instructed;

And inasmuch as they sinned they might be chastened, that they might repent;

And inasmuch as they were humble they might be made strong, and blessed from on high, and receive knowledge from time to time. (D&C 1.24-28.)

On the missionary spirit:
Now behold, a marvelous work is about to come forth among the children of men.

Therefore, O ye that embark in the service of God, see that ye serve him with all your heart, might, mind and strength, that ye may stand blameless before God at the last day.

Therefore, if ye have desires to serve God ye are called to the work;

For behold the field is white already to harvest; and lo, he that thrusteth in his sickle with his might, the same layeth up in store that he perisheth not, but bringeth salvation to his soul;

And faith, hope, charity and love, with an eye single to the glory of God, qualify him for the work.

Remember faith, virtue, knowledge, temperance, patience, brotherly kindness, godliness, charity, humility, diligence.

Ask, and ye shall receive; knock, and it shall be opened to you. Amen. (D&C 4.)

On Jesus:

Learn of me, and listen to my words; walk in the meekness of my Spirit, and you shall have peace in me. (D&C 19:23.)

But learn that he who doeth the works of righteousness shall receive his reward, even peace in this world, and eternal life in the world to come. (D&C 59:23.)

And if your eye be single to my glory, your whole bodies shall be filled with light, and there shall be no darkness in you; and that body which is filled with light comprehendeth all things.

Therefore, sanctify yourselves that your minds become single to God, and the days will come that you shall see him; for he will unveil his face unto you, and it shall be in his own time, and in his own way, and according to his own will. (D&C 88:67-68.)

On baptism:

All those who humble themselves before God, and desire to be baptized, and come forth with broken hearts and contrite spirits, and witness before the church that they have truly repented of all their sins, and are willing to take upon them the name of Jesus Christ, having a determination to serve him to the end, and truly manifest by their works that they have received of the Spirit of Christ unto the remission of their sins, shall be received by baptism into his church. (D&C 20:37.)

There are whole sections in the Doctrine and Covenants that inspire the reader for their language as well as ideas. Read sections 76, 88, and 93 for glimpses of eternal life. The Word of Wisdom in section 89 is remarkable for its restraint, wisdom, and tone. The finest statement in any scripture on the spirit of the priesthood and how authority should be exercised is found in section 121. Written to the saints while the Prophet Joseph Smith was in Liberty Jail, it is remarkable for its depth, optimism, and force. (Read D&C 121:34-46.)

The Pearl of Great Price

The Pearl of Great Price, by far the briefest of the standard works, contains many things that are especially appealing because of the way they are stated. For example:

Joseph Smith's own story is noteworthy for the simple, sincere, and detailed account of his remarkable spiritual experiences.

The Articles of Faith, while not a complete statement of Church beliefs, is a clear and substantive presentation of many basic tenets of the Church.

I am particularly inspired by Moses, chapter one, which portrays the infinite creations of the Father and Son and declares God's purpose in these memorable words: "For behold, this is my work and my glory—to bring to pass the immortality and eternal life of man." (Moses 1:39.)

10

Understanding the Old Testament

What is distinctive about the Old Testament? In what order should the thirty-nine books of this scripture be read? What should we look for as we read them?

The Old Testament is three times as large as the New Testament and about twice as large as the Book of Mormon. It also has the greatest number of authors, many of them anonymous. As a whole it is the most ancient of scriptures, having been written over a thousand-year period before the time of Christ. As noted in chapter 9, the Old Testament is the greatest literary scripture we have, both in amount and in variety. What in other scriptures can compare, from a literary point of view, with the book of Job? No other scripture is so rich in biographical study as the Old Testament. One who reads and studies it feels he knows a good deal about Abraham, Jacob, Joseph, Samson, Moses, Saul, David, Ruth, and Elijah. Novels, plays, oratorios, paintings, and pictures have been produced around these characters. As our oldest scripture, the Old Testament is richest in human interest and experience.

A most appreciated characteristic of the Old Testament's portrayal of characters is its honesty and candor. Some writers cover up the humanity of their religious leaders. Not so with Old Testament authors. They tell of

Jacob's deception toward Esau, Isaac, and Laban, as well as his strength of character. Moses, revered as the greatest among the prophets and as the spiritual founder of his nation, takes honors unto himself that belonged to God. (See Numbers 20:10-13 and Deuteronomy 32:48-52.) And David, Israel's idyllic king who defeated the whole of Canaan in battle, is portrayed as a murderer and an adulterer—and in the end, as a pathetic old man. Saul, Israel's first king, ends his career in madness, while Solomon ends his in utter folly. In fact, most of the kings of Israel and Judah are described as having done "evil in the sight of the Lord."

The Old Testament tells the story of a great nation and people established by a covenant between God and Abraham, that heroic, generous man of faith. The covenant continued through Isaac and Jacob and was renewed again with Moses. What a giant was Moses—prophet, leader, and lawgiver! He has provided a legacy of strength and direction to Israel for over three millennia.

The Old Testament was the first scripture to put a *personal* God in the heart of history—guiding, blessing, chastising, and trying to fulfill his purposes through a chosen people. As a nation, ancient Israel failed Jehovah—but Israel left us, through her prophets and writers, a clear picture of what God demands of any people worthy of his name, and the hope that mankind may one day learn to walk more uprightly before him.

The Old Testament is a rich mixture of some of the worst and the best of ethical standards. Except in Paul's writings, no other scripture condones slavery (see Philemon), none describes atrocities as God-approved, or blesses men in their deceit (i.e., Jacob). In contrast, there is no higher ethical demand made of a people in any scripture than we find in the teachings of the writing prophets and in much of the law of Moses. Old Testament ethical teachings are overwhelmingly good—remarkably so, considering the times and the cultures of surrounding peoples.

How to Read the Old Testament

To understand the history in the Old Testament one should read its books in the following sequence:

Genesis	A great book of biographies and narratives
Exodus	The story of the Exodus from Egypt with Moses as the leading character
Numbers	Exodus continued
Leviticus	A remarkable code of ethics in chapters 19-26
Deuteronomy	The second statement of the law
Joshua	A period of political instability and near defeat
Judges	The struggle to conquer Canaan continues after Joshua
1 and 2 Samuel	The prophetic leadership of Samuel; the reigns of Saul and David
1 and 2 Kings	The reign of Solomon, the history of Israel and Judah to the Assyrian captivity of Israel (722 B.C.) and the Babylonian destruction of Jerusalem (586 B.C.)

The greatest of the writing prophets fall into this period just before and during the defeat of the two kingdoms. They should be studied as a group and in conjunction with the political history described in 1 and 2 Kings.

Amos, 760 B.C.   To the northern kingdom

Hosea, 740 B.C.   To the northern kingdom

Isaiah, 740–700 B.C.   To both Israel and Judah, but mainly to Judah

Micah, 730–700 B.C.   To Judah

Zephaniah, 626 B.C.   To Judah

Nahum, 612 B.C.   To Judah

Jeremiah, 626–   To Judah
586 B.C.

Habakkuk,   Concern for Judah
608–597 B.C.

Ezekiel, 597–550 B.C.   Prophet to Judah in Babylon

Zechariah, 520–   Prophets in Judah after the
519 B.C.   return of some Jews from
Haggai, 520–519 B.C.   Persia to Palestine in 538
Malachi, 475–450 B.C.   B.C.
Obadiah, 450–400 B.C.
Joel, 400 B.C.
Jonah, 350 (?) B.C.

The theme common to most of the writing prophets is called ethical monotheism. For them there is one God, and he is a person of justice, impartiality, and mercy. He demands that his followers also practice justice and mercy in their relations with each other. Without these ethical relationships religious rituals, offerings, hymns, and prayers are vain, hypocritical, and completely unacceptable. No other group of men at any time in history has written so powerfully and beautifully on the essential role of ethics in the everyday life of society. Amos, Hosea, Isaiah, Micah, and Jeremiah are particularly powerful voices in the cause of righteousness.

Ezekiel went with the captives to Babylon, where he did a remarkable thing to preserve the religion of his people. Until then, in Canaan the Israelite faith had been identified largely with the nation and with a holy land. Ezekiel placed religion on a more personal basis. A Jew could please God anywhere, under any conditions, if he would learn and live God's laws.

The Jews called the third group of books in the Old Testament the Writings. As previously stated, the Writings were canonized late in Jewish history, not until about A.D. 150, and they were never considered as authoritative as the Law and the Prophets. But they contain such choice writings as the Psalms and the wisdom literature: Proverbs, Ecclesiastes, and Job.

Proverbs is a positive, optimistic collection of wise admonitions. These encourage sound and practical virtues such as respect for God and parents, industry, and cheerfulness—and they warn against wild women and wine. Particularly impressive are the chapters that extol wisdom (3, 4, and 8) and one that describes the ideal Hebrew woman (31). The ideal Hebrew woman lived for her husband and her household and worked from dawn into the night. There is no mention of her social or cultural life, aspects of living important to women of our time.

Ecclesiastes is quite different from Proverbs; it is more realistic, the fruit of a mind that had probably reviewed one thousand years of Israelite history. The theme here is "all is vanity" (futility). Even so, Ecclesiastes has a stoic and positive bit of advice. People are encouraged to enjoy work and family and to keep the commandments of

God (see, for example, 9:7-11 and 12:13-14). The book is beautifully and interestingly written.

Some scholars have said that the book of Job is the greatest piece of religious literature ever penned by man. Surely it is a work of art, great in thought and language. The core question is, why do men suffer? Was Job being punished for his sins as his so-called friends argued, or does suffering have a deeper, unknown meaning? After three rounds of eloquent debate, the voice of God speaks out of the whirlwind. His wrath is "kindled against" Job's friends because they had "not spoken of me [God] the thing that is right" (42:7). Suffering is not necessarily punishment for sin. Job learned too that he had uttered "words without knowledge." Who was he to judge the ways of the Almighty? Job learned that he must walk by faith and trust in the wisdom of God. Job was not criticized for questioning the justice of his Maker, nor for his cries of despair.

The Psalms, loved by Jew and Christian alike, should be read, not for doctrine, but for inspiration in a spirit of worship. They bring peace and comfort to the believer. Note, for example, the following:

8th	What is man?
23rd	The Lord is my shepherd.
24th	Who shall ascend into the hill of the Lord?
51st	Create in me a clean heart.
73rd	Whom have I in heaven but thee?
139th	Whither shall I flee from thy presence?

Nehemiah and Ezra tell of the rebuilding of Judah and the second temple after Cyrus of Persia permitted Jews to return to the land of Canaan in 538 B.C. Their writings are very interesting historically. Their leadership enabled Judaism to survive and, through the heroic efforts of the Maccabees, prepare the setting for the ministry of Jesus.

The Old Testament is the most difficult of all scripture to understand. Help is needed from Bible commentaries and scholars to comprehend its historical background.

11

Understanding the New Testament

The New Testament is an interesting, exciting, and inspiring scripture because it is centered in the life, teachings, and mission of Jesus of Nazareth. This scripture portrays him in all of his humanity and divinity. We see him as a man among human beings, a person of great compassion for the poor, the afflicted, and the despised. We note how he astonished his hearers by speaking with authority, with great insight, with simplicity and profundity, beauty and grace. He was followed by disciples, by the multitudes, and even by critics and enemies. He stirred the minds and hearts of every class in society.

The New Testament also portrays Jesus as the Son of God, heralded at birth and triumphant in death, rising from the grave to electrify his disciples and to give hope to mankind. We see his miraculous power to heal the sick, to raise the dead, and most of all to change the hearts of men—to turn a fisherman like Peter and a Pharisee like Saul into men of God.

The twenty-seven books of the New Testament were written over a period of about one hundred years—roughly from A.D. 50 to 150—by men who either knew Christ or had access to earlier written records and to oral traditions about him. The authors not only knew the Savior or people who knew him, but they also believed and loved him.

Luke, the physician and companion of Paul, wrote two of the choicest books in the New Testament—his Gospel and the book of Acts. Luke probably never knew the Savior personally, but he, like any good historian, had many earlier written records at hand. He begins his Gospel in this way:

> Forasmuch as many have taken in hand to set forth in order a declaration of those things which are most surely believed among us,
>
> Even as they delivered them unto us, which from the beginning were eyewitnesses, and ministers of the word;
>
> It seemed good to me also, having had perfect understanding of all things from the very first, to write unto thee in order, most excellent Theophilus,
>
> That thou mightest know the certainty of those things, wherein thou hast been instructed. (Luke 1:1-4.)

Luke proceeds to write a Gospel that is unexcelled—a moving, joyous, triumphant biography of Jesus.

The Books of the New Testament

This scripture falls into a five-fold grouping as follows:

The Gospels	Biographies of Jesus
The Book of Acts	The rise of the Christian Church
The Epistles of Paul	To particular branches and persons
The Universal Epistles	To the Church at large
Revelation	Depicting the triumph of Christ and the Church

The word *gospel* means "good news" or "glad tidings." The first three Gospels are called synoptic because they have basically the same character and arrangement. Matthew and Luke begin with Jesus' birth, whereas Mark begins with Jesus' ministry as introduced by John the Baptist. All three end with the story of Christ's resurrection. The Gospel of John is of a different character. It begins by declaring the Savior's Godhood. In the Gospel of John incidents in his life are repeatedly told to illustrate his divinity.

In what order should we read the New Testament? The Gospel of Mark is the earliest written Gospel. It has been called a diamond in the rough, being less polished and briefer than the other Gospels. For these reasons I suggest that one begin reading the New Testament with Mark, followed by Matthew, Luke, and John in that order.

Matthew has been called the teaching Gospel because it contains some rather extended sayings of Jesus. It is here that we find the Sermon on the Mount in one piece, chapters 5, 6, and 7. Chapter 23 is a long speech critical of scribes and Pharisees. The whole Gospel of Matthew is rich in the Savior's teaching.

Luke is a beautifully written Gospel. It tells the story of Christ's birth and his resurrection in exquisite language and with exultation. Luke also contains the most parables, including some choice ones not found in the other Gospels. (Read, for example, Luke 10 and 15.) Luke may have written his Gospel with the gentile world in mind, given the book's broad and universal appeal and graceful style.

The Gospel of John is more theological and symbolic than the Synoptic Gospels. John quotes Jesus as saying, "I am the bread of life," "I am the true vine," "I am the way, the truth, and the life." His Gospel is profound and certainly beautiful in its own original way.

The book of Acts is the most historical of the twenty-seven New Testament books. It tells the exciting story of the rise of the pristine Church—first in Palestine under the leadership of Peter (chapters 1-8 and 10-12), and then in the gentile world through the missionary labors of Paul (chapters 9 and 13-28). Peter and Paul loom large in heroic roles, and the whole Christian movement is seen in its glorious and miraculous beginnings. Acts should be read after the Gospels. Written by Luke, it is a continuation of his Gospel.

The epistles of Paul were written, it is believed, before any other books of the New Testament. Other writings on which the Gospels were based were likely extant before Paul's writings, but his are the earliest of the books preserved in the New Testament. Most of Paul's epistles were written to branches of the early Church that he had founded. Word would come to him of conditions in a branch, and he would respond with greetings, admonitions, encouragement, and instruction as the situation suggested. The following are his epistles to branches: 1 and 2 Thessalonians, Galatians, Philippians, Colossians, 1 and 2 Corinthians, and Ephesians.

Paul also wrote four epistles to individuals: 1 and 2 Timothy, Titus, and Philemon.

The epistle to Philemon is a one-page plea for him to forgive his runaway former slave, Onesimus, and to accept him as a brother in Christ. It is an unusual and beautiful epistle.

Written neither to a branch nor to an individual, Paul's epistle to the Romans, the most difficult of his letters, was written to the Church at large. It contains the fullest statement of his theology.

The last group of letters, the universal epistles, include James, 1, 2, and 3 John, 1 and 2 Peter, Jude, and Hebrews. These epistles, unlike most of Paul's, were not written to a particular branch or person, but to all Christians.

James is a very practical book, typified by this statement: "Pure religion and undefiled before God and the Father is this, To visit the fatherless and widows in their affliction, and to keep himself unspotted from the world." (James 1:27.)

The letters known as 1, 2, and 3 John are beautiful epistles that encourage Christians to love one another.

First John is the longest and richest of the three and merits repeated reading and study. The epistles we call 1 and 2 Peter are rich in instruction and encouragement to the early saints who suffered persecution and affliction. I especially enjoy the following lines from 2 Peter:

> Whereby are given unto us exceeding great and precious promises: that by these ye might be partakers of the divine nature, having escaped the corruption that is in the world through lust.
> And beside this, giving all diligence, add to your faith virtue; and to virtue knowledge;
> And to knowledge temperance; and to temperance patience; and to patience godliness;
> And to godliness brotherly kindness; and to brotherly kindness charity.
> For if these things be in you, and abound, they make you that ye shall neither be barren nor unfruitful in the knowledge of our Lord Jesus Christ. (2 Peter 1:4-8.)

Jude is a warning to the saints not to be led astray by dissenters and destroyers of the Christian faith. "Keep yourselves in the love of God, looking for the mercy of our Lord Jesus Christ unto eternal life." (Jude 1:21.)

Hebrews, ascribed to Paul in the heading, is now believed by most scholars not to have been written by the apostle. It does not read as his other epistles do. Be that as it may, Hebrews is original in its witness of Christ, its recital of faith, and its encouragement to live the good life.

Revelation is a most difficult book, highly symbolic, often misunderstood, but with beautiful passages. It portrays the triumph of Christ over the power of Rome. It needs to be read with a good Bible commentary at hand. And even then one should not expect to understand it all.

The New Testament makes delightful and inspiring reading because of its rejoicing in the ministry and mission of Jesus Christ. It is a triumphant work that can be studied for both information and inspiration. It is the devotional classic of Christianity.

12

Understanding the
Book of Mormon

The Book of Mormon is the most unusual scripture in the way the original record was kept, preserved, and translated. It is unique in its content; no other scripture is so miraculous in character. No other scripture is so misunderstood and misinterpreted as the Book of Mormon. It is considered by many to be a history of the American Indian, a guide to archaeology of the Americas, and/or pure dictation from God. It is none of these. We should let the book speak for itself.

The Book of Mormon is not a history of the pre-Columbian American Indian. Its history ends about A.D. 420. It does not describe what happened in the Western Hemisphere between 420 and 1492, nor does it tell of other immigrants who may have come to the American continent before, after, or even during the Book of Mormon period. We should not assume that all Native Americans are necessarily descendants of Lamanites.

This scripture describes three small groups that came to the Western Hemisphere: the Jaredites, then the Lehi colony, and then the Mulekites. It mentions no one else. Other peoples may have come across the Bering Strait, from Europe, or even from the isles of the Pacific before, during, or after the Book of Mormon period.

The Book of Mormon is not a geographical text. It

contains no maps. Places and movements are named not for their own sake, but are incidental to other subject matter. Locations are given only in relative terms. Writers who wish to make a geography text out of the Book of Mormon only confuse the issue.

The Book of Mormon is not a text in anthropology or archaeology. Many apologists for the Book of Mormon have tried to establish its authenticity through archaeological data, but they have erred in two ways: (1) most have not been trained in these sciences, and therefore they cannot and do not use scientific data accurately and honestly, and (2) many have failed to recognize the point made above that the Book of Mormon does not claim to be a total history of ancient cultures and civilizations in America. Writers and speakers who identify every ruin in the Americas with the Book of Mormon account are on shaky ground. They may be unfair to the book, if not actually misleading. How, may I ask, does one distinguish Book of Mormon artifacts and ruins from those belonging to other ancient sojourners on the American continent?

One summer I took a class at the University of Washington in the archaeology and anthropology of the Americas. My purpose was to compare the findings of these sciences with data in the Book of Mormon. I studied the subject eagerly and arduously, taking careful note of anything that might relate to the Book of Mormon. When the course was over, I hid out and read the Book of Mormon through again, looking for related data. It was then that I came to realize for the first time what this scripture really is—a profoundly religious record.

No, the Book of Mormon is not history, geography, or archaeology; rather it is essentially a religious record, a witness that Jesus is the Christ and a plea to men and women to repent and to bear one another's burdens. There is a historical perspective in the book, but it acts only as a frame for a religious picture. Book of Mormon authors were devout men who wrote of things sacred and important to them.

The Book of Mormon is an *abridged, religious* account. As Mormon and Moroni abridged (cut or reduced) the account, they apparently made it even more religious in emphasis than the original record may have been. To get the most out of reading this scripture, we should read it with the same interest as the authors had in writing it. Moroni was quite right when he admonished the reader to ask God in the name of Christ if his record were true, and the truth would be made manifest by the Holy Ghost. (Moroni 10:3-6.)

How to Read the Book of Mormon

In reading the Book of Mormon, begin at the beginning and read it straight through. The book of Ether, near the end, is out of place chronologically, but this is not important. The main thrust of the story begins and continues with the Lehi colony, particularly with the conflict between the Nephites and the Lamanites.

As you read, do not look for perfection. We believe the Book of Mormon to be the word of God. It is a divinely inspired record, but it is given in man's language and weakness that he might come to an understanding.

It is not written, either in the original or in its translation, in modern English. Therefore, it may be difficult to understand in places.

I find it, for the most part, easy to understand and unsophisticated in its teaching, so much so that many of its finest insights are overlooked. For example, the following three passages have come to be very meaningful to me. They grow meaningful out of experience and have value for us today.

1. In Jacob 4:10 we read: "Seek not to counsel the Lord, but to take counsel from his hand. For behold, ye yourselves know that he counseleth in wisdom, and in justice, and in great mercy, over all his works." If we believe in God we should not seek to bend his will to conform to our desires; rather, we should learn his will and conform our lives to his principles and purposes.

My son, when he was three years old, climbed on a tractor, fell off, kicked the tractor, and said, "Daddy, I don't like that tractor." In like manner, many of us, even in adulthood, seek to counsel life instead of learning sound principles and conforming our lives to them. We fail to accept reality.

2. In Alma 32 we read about Alma's straight talk to a community of Nephites who were humbled because of their "exceeding poverty." Alma pointed out that they had been brought to their humility by circumstance. Then he proceeded to make a fine and significant distinction between being compelled to be humble and becoming humble through the word of God:

"And now, because ye are compelled to be humble blessed are ye; for a man sometimes, if he is compelled to be humble, seeketh repentance. . . . And now, as I said unto you, that because ye were compelled to be humble ye were blessed, do ye not suppose that they are more blessed who truly humble themselves because of the word?" (Alma 32:13, 14.)

Poverty may bring a person to repentance, as Alma says, but not always. At other times it can cause bitterness, cynicism, even hate. When circumstances induce humility, one never knows whether the apparent humility is genuine or forced, whereas a person whose humility is born of the love of God and Christ and fellow human beings is genuinely humble within himself. How much of our religious life is within us, and how much is externally compelled?

3. I was a missionary in Germany after World War I, and postwar inflation had wrecked the economy of that country. As we tracted from door to door and talked with people who had been through those prolonged, devastating experiences, we found that many had become atheistic and cynical, while others had become remarkably humble and compassionate. When I read about the Nephites' reaction to decades of bitter fighting between themselves and the Lamanites—"But behold, because of the exceeding great length of the war between the

Nephites and Lamanites many had become hardened
. . . and many were softened because of their afflictions,
insomuch that they did humble themselves before God,
even in the depth of humility" (Alma 62:41)—I thought
how true to life this was! I have since observed many
others who have suffered through the furnace of affliction. They either come out burned, scarred, and mean in
disposition, or gentle, humble, and refined.

The Book of Mormon can teach us much about living
if we have eyes to see. The following passages give us
reason to contemplate:

2 Nephi 2	Purpose and nature of life— "Men are that they might have joy" but in a world of good and evil, of opposites
2 Nephi 26	The impartiality of God
2 Nephi 28	Rationalization, continuous revelation
Jacob 2	Pride, brotherhood, chastity
Enos	The power and fruits of prayer
Mosiah 18	The finest statement in any scripture on baptism
Mosiah 29	The values of democracy; the evils of a dictatorship
Alma 5 and 7	Beautiful pleas to repent
Alma 29:1-8	Tolerance, broadmindedness
Alma 32	Great chapter on faith

Alma 34	Atonement, repentance
Alma 37:33-37 and 38:10-14	Counsel to missionaries
Alma 40	Life after death
3 Nephi 9:17-22	The Christian life
3 Nephi 12, 13, 14	The Sermon on the Mount with significant changes
3 Nephi 18	The meaning of the sacrament
4 Nephi	A Christian community
Mormon 8	A sense of values
Moroni 4 and 5	Meaningful sacramental prayers
Moroni 6	Life in the Church of Christ
Moroni 7	The goodness of God
Moroni 8	Infant baptism and first principles and ordinances
Moroni 10	Moroni's heartfelt plea and farewell

A fine Jewish friend who had read the New Testament asked me, "Why does one need the Book of Mormon if he believes in the New Testament?" I answered that the Book of Mormon contains very few teachings that cannot be found in either the Old or New Testament. In fact, it reinforces and underscores biblical teachings. But it does present another witness of another people, a witness that God lives, that Jesus is the Christ, that revelation is continuous, and that the basic Judeo-Christian standards of conduct are viable. I also told him that the Book of Mormon gives added meaning to the basic principles and ordinances of the gospel. In no other scripture do we find a description of the growth and fruits of faith as in Alma 32. Alma's cries of repentance are original and moving. In fact, repentance is the basic theme of the book.

Baptism also is explained more fully and more beautifully in this scripture than it is in the New Testament or any other scripture. Mosiah 18 is a remarkable chapter on the subject, particularly as it speaks of man's contribution to the covenant. All references to baptism in the Book of Mormon are consistent with each other. They stress what we can give to God through this ordinance even more than what we may receive. The Book of Mormon contains two sacramental prayers of rich content and it gives the meaning of the sacrament as a memorial to the Savior.

In simple, clear language the Book of Mormon adds immeasurably to our understanding of the gospel and church of Jesus Christ.

13

Understanding the Doctrine and Covenants

What are the distinctive characteristics of the Doctrine and Covenants? How does it differ from the other standard works? It is the only scripture that is wholly modern, containing writings from 1823 to 1978. It is the only scripture that has come to English-speaking people in their own language. It is largely the work of one author, Joseph Smith, which makes for unity of style. Its content is also quite distinctive; it is the only scripture relating directly to the restoration of the gospel and the Church.

The Doctrine and Covenants has much in common with the other standard works. Like other scriptures, it is a collection of writings given over time under diverse circumstances. Each section should be read by itself with knowledge of the historical background. Each revelation was a response to a need, and to earnest inquiry by the Prophet Joseph.

Section 121, for example, on the spirit of the priesthood, is all the more remarkable if one realizes that it was received while the Prophet was suffering the misery and indignities of Liberty Jail in Missouri. The Word of Wisdom was the Lord's response to the temperance movement in Ohio, which attracted the prophet's attention.

The Spirit of the Doctrine and Covenants

The message of the Doctrine and Covenants, although addressed primarily to the Saints and their leaders, is also spoken to all the world. Like Micah of old who cried, "Hear, all ye people; hearken, O earth, and all that therein is" (Micah 1:2), the Doctrine and Covenants speaks to all people: "For verily the voice of the Lord is unto all men, and there is none to escape; and there is no eye that shall not see, neither ear that shall not hear, neither heart that shall not be penetrated. . . . And the voice of warning shall be unto all people." (D&C 1:2, 4.)

Furthermore, there is no question about the eventual success of the restoration movement. It is God's work and he will prevail. No hand will stay him. "The works, and the designs, and the purposes of God cannot be frustrated, neither can they come to naught. . . . Remember, remember that it is not the work of God that is frustrated, but the work of men." (D&C 3:1, 3.)

The Doctrine and Covenants is marked by an overriding confidence, a spirit of positive action. Even in the darkest hours of Mormon history, there is no ultimate despair. Anyone who would join the cause must be a partaker of that spirit.

"Verily I say, men should be anxiously engaged in a good cause, and do many things of their own free will, and bring to pass much righteousness; For the power is in them, wherein they are agents unto themselves." (D&C 58:27-28.)

Some Distinctive Teachings of the Doctrine and Covenants

In the early history of The Church of Jesus Christ of Latter-day Saints, new members and leaders were in great need of divine guidance, and they sought it eagerly and earnestly. The Doctrine and Covenants is a partial record of revelations received throughout Church history. Many of the revelations therein are directed to individuals and are thus repeated. Others apply more to the Church at large and have universal and lasting significance. Some of the original and significant themes developed in this scripture are discussed as follows:

1. *Priesthood and Church government.* Priesthood is barely mentioned in the New Testament, but the subject is developed at length and in considerable detail in the Doctrine and Covenants. There we learn that priesthood is a real, objective, divine authority delegated to man by ordination from those who received it from Christ and his servants. There is one priesthood divided into two divisions, Melchizedek and Aaronic, each with various callings.

One of the unique features of the Mormon doctrine of priesthood is the organization of quorums. Every man holding the priesthood, including the president of the Church, belongs to a quorum or a body of priesthood holders. Quorums provide counsel and wisdom, cultivate brotherhood, teach doctrine, train members in priesthood duties, and give opportunity for spiritual and practical service. The quorum is an ingenious arrangement that greatly enlarges the functions and meaning of the priesthood.

The duties of the various quorums and offices in the priesthood are quite clearly outlined and are remarkably current. There is a definite hierarchy of authority in the Church, headed by the First Presidency and the prophet. This concentration of authority is balanced by a number of features that guard against its misuse. No man is to hold any office in the Church without the consent of those whom he serves. Church officers are sustained regularly in their callings. Moreover, since the priesthood is available to all worthy males over twelve, and since there are so many quorums and callings, there is a great sharing of priesthood functions and power.

Most remarkable to me is Doctrine and Covenants 121, which describes in beautiful language the spirit in which divine authority should and can operate. Portions of it are quoted below:

> Behold, there are many called, but few are chosen. And why are they not chosen?
>
> Because their hearts are set so much upon the things of this world, and aspire to the honors of men, that they do not learn this one lesson—
>
> That the rights of the priesthood are inseparably connected with the powers of heaven, and that the powers of heaven cannot be controlled nor handled only upon the principles of righteousness.
>
> That they may be conferred upon us, it is true; but when we undertake to cover our sins, or to gratify our pride, our vain ambition, or to exercise control or dominion or compulsion upon the souls of the children of men, in any degree of unrighteousness, behold, the heavens withdraw themselves; the Spirit of the Lord is grieved; and when it is withdrawn, Amen to the priesthood or the authority of that man.
>
> Behold, ere he is aware, he is left unto himself, to kick against the pricks, to persecute the saints, and to fight against God.
>
> We have learned by sad experience that it is the nature and disposition of almost all men, as soon as they get a little authority, as they suppose, they will immediately begin to exercise unrighteous dominion.
>
> Hence many are called, but few are chosen.
>
> No power or influence can or ought to be maintained by virtue of the priesthood, only by persuasion, by long-suffering, by gentleness and meekness, and by love unfeigned;
>
> By kindness, and pure knowledge, which shall greatly enlarge the soul without hypocrisy, and without guile—
>
> Reproving betimes with sharpness, when moved upon by the Holy Ghost; and then showing forth afterwards an increase of love toward him whom thou hast reproved, lest he esteem thee to be his enemy;
>
> That he may know that thy faithfulness is stronger than the cords of death.
>
> Let thy bowels also be full of charity towards all men, and to the household of faith, and let virtue garnish thy thoughts unceasingly; then shall thy confidence wax strong in the presence of God; and the doctrine of the priesthood shall distil upon thy soul as the dews from heaven.
>
> The Holy Ghost shall be thy constant companion, and thy scepter an unchanging scepter of righteousness and truth; and

thy dominion shall be an everlasting dominion, and without compulsory means it shall flow unto thee forever and ever. (D&C 121:34-46.)

For further study of the contribution of the Doctrine and Covenants to our understanding of the priesthood, read sections 2, 13, 20, 84, 107, and 121. Section 107 is particularly comprehensive and explicit in outlining the quorums of the priesthood and their respective authority.

2. *Cooperation in economic matters.* The restoration was not only to prepare people for salvation in the life to come but to transform human beings here and now that they might be fit for the kingdom of God. Early in Church history Joseph Smith received revelations outlining what is known as the law of consecration. Members were to deed all they owned to the Lord (through the bishop) and receive back a stewardship that they would operate as their own, giving surpluses back to the Church for communal purposes and to bless the poor, widows, and orphans. The revelations admonished:

". . . in your temporal things you shall be equal, and this not grudgingly, otherwise the abundance of the manifestations of the Spirit shall be withheld." (D&C 70:14.) "For if ye are not equal in earthly things ye cannot be equal in obtaining heavenly things." (D&C 78:6.)

Much of the Doctrine and Covenants is an inspiring record of the Church's heroic effort to establish a consecrated society. Due to persecution and human frailties, the undertaking failed, but it has left a will to cooperate and sacrifice for the Church and each other that is still present among Latter-day Saints to a marked degree.

3. *Health.* The Word of Wisdom (section 89) is a remarkable document on healthful living—remarkable for its measured tone, for its anticipation of the deceit and unhealthful practices of our time, for its very sound specific guides to healthful living, and for its divine inspiration. Many Latter-day Saints have yet to learn that it was given "for a principle," and that some of its

finest features are its emphasis on things we should do, such as the eating of herbs and fruits in the season thereof and partaking of all good things with "prudence and thanksgiving."

4. *Missionary work.* The Doctrine and Covenants places great emphasis on missionary work and contains inspiring passages on why and how missionary service should be rendered:

> Remember the worth of souls is great in the sight of God;
> For, behold, the Lord your Redeemer suffered death in the flesh; wherefore he suffered the pain of all men, that all men might repent and come unto him.
> And he hath risen again from the dead, that he might bring all men unto him, on conditions of repentance.
> And how great is his joy in the soul that repenteth!
> Wherefore, you are called to cry repentance unto this people.
> And if it so be that you should labor all your days in crying repentance unto this people, and bring, save it be one soul unto me, how great shall be your joy with him in the kingdom of my Father!
> And now, if your joy will be great with one soul that you have brought unto me into the kingdom of my Father, how great will be your joy if you should bring many souls unto me! (D&C 18:10-16.)

> Therefore, O ye that embark in the service of God, see that ye serve him with all your heart, might, mind and strength, that ye may stand blameless before God at the last day.
> Therefore, if ye have desires to serve God ye are called to the work;
> For behold the field is white already to harvest; and lo, he that thrusteth in his sickle with his might, the same layeth up in store that he perisheth not, but bringeth salvation to his soul;
> And faith, hope, charity and love, with an eye single to the glory of God, qualify him for the work.
> Remember faith, virtue, knowledge, temperance, patience, brotherly kindness, godliness, charity, humility, diligence.
> Ask, and ye shall receive; knock, and it shall be opened unto you. Amen. (D&C 4:2-7.)

5. *New doctrines.* The Doctrine and Covenants throws new light on theology. Several sections describe

man's unlimited potential to share in the work and glory of God. Sections 76, 88, 93, 110, and 132 teach the unique Mormon doctrine of eternal progression or the possibility of achieving a more God-like life. The Doctrine and Covenants verifies that man is truly in the image of his heavenly Father, and no limits are placed on his future self-realization as a child of that great Being.

Section 93 declares that "intelligence . . . was not created or made" and is free "to act for itself." "The elements are eternal" too. This bold doctrine makes man responsible for his own actions. It also relieves God of the responsibility for evil, since he did not create all things ultimately but has had to work with coeternal, self-existing entities—intelligences and elements and the laws that govern them.

14

Understanding the Pearl of Great Price

The Pearl of Great Price is the shortest and most recent scripture to become one of the standard works of the Church. Elder Franklin D. Richards of the Council of the Twelve first published it, along with other revelations, as a missionary booklet in Liverpool, England, in 1851. The present Pearl of Great Price was accepted as scripture by the Church in 1902.

The Pearl of Great Price is unique in that it combines three ancient writings: the Book of Moses, the Book of Abraham, and Matthew 23:39 and chapter 24, with two modern writings—extracts from the history of the Prophet Joseph Smith and the Articles of Faith.

Distinctive Teachings

The Book of Moses is based on Genesis with interesting additions. Chapter one tells of the endless creations of God by the power of his Son for the purpose of "bringing to pass the immortality and eternal life of man." Thus it portrays a God who is forever creative, and unselfishly so, in the interest of his children. Fascinating too is the remark of Moses, who, having had a vision of God and some of his creations, cried: "Now, for this cause I know that man is nothing, which thing I never had supposed." (Moses 1:10.) Moments later, Satan appeared and asked Moses to worship him. Moses then, in true perspective, said to Satan: "Who art thou? . . . that I should worship thee? . . . for God said unto me: Thou art after the similitude of mine Only Begotten." (Moses 1:13, 16.)

Chapter 4 of Moses is original in describing a council in heaven wherein Jesus Christ was chosen to come to earth to redeem mankind. Heavenly Father's plan to respect the free agency of man was accepted, whereas Lucifer's plan to coerce man into salvation was rejected—perhaps because it was unworkable as well as motivated in search of self-glory.

The high point of the Book of Abraham is found in the third chapter, which compares the intelligences with the stars of heaven, numerous and varying in degree of light. The intelligences of men are not equal—and likely never were—and God is more intelligent than all of them. But man is not unlike God and is only different in degree. Man has divine qualities in embryo and can look to God as the person to emulate and to follow.

Even in our pre-earth life, the spirits who were to become men and women in the flesh were unequal. Abraham and others merited leadership roles and were chosen, foreordained, to their missions in mortality. One, Jesus Christ, "was like unto God." He assumed a creative, redeeming role in behalf of human beings. He prepared the earth where the spirit children of God could live in mortality, prove themselves, and add glory to their eternal lives.

The third chapter of Abraham is full of inspiration and motivation. It glorifies man without in any way detracting from the glory of the Father and the Son.

Joseph Smith—History, subtitled "Extracts from the History of Joseph Smith, the Prophet," is commonly called "Joseph Smith's Own Story." It is told simply and clearly, giving considerable detail, and it has the ring of sincerity and truth. Central to the story is the vision of the Father and the Son, two living persons who spoke to

Joseph and of whom he reverently states: ". . . whose brightness and glory defy all description."

The Articles of Faith were written in 1841–42 as part of a letter Joseph Smith wrote in response to John Wentworth, a Chicago newspaper editor, who was writing the history of Vermont and wished to include something about the Prophet, who was born there.

The Articles of Faith are not a complete statement of Latter-day Saint beliefs, but they are a substantial listing of some of our basic principles. Dr. James E. Talmage's book on the subject illustrates how meaningful they are. The Articles of Faith are varied in character. The first nine have to do with theology and our faith in the Church and its authority. Articles ten through thirteen express our attitude toward the building of Zion, tolerance for other faiths, and obedience to law, and they conclude with encouragement of an open-ended search for "anything virtuous, lovely, or of good report or praiseworthy."

15

How to Study Scripture

In previous chapters, the nature of scripture, guidelines to its interpretation, comments on its beauty, and introduction of the reader to each standard work relative to its uniqueness and special contributions have been discussed. In conclusion, a few additional ideas on how to study the scriptures are suggested.

1. *Make the scriptures your own.* Read them for what they can teach you about how to live, what to believe, how to serve God and man. Take a colored pencil and underline things that impress you.

My father, Milton Bennion, went on a mission to New Zealand as an eighteen-year-old youth. This was in the early history of the mission. Much of the work was among Maoris. Father told of being confined alone in a cabin during heavy, perpetual rain for weeks. Natives brought him potatoes twice a day; his other nourishment came from reading the New Testament by candlelight. He practically memorized it.

He also internalized its teachings. I have known no man with more integrity, moral courage, humility, and love for all men and women than my father. He made the New Testament his own. He became a true disciple of Jesus Christ.

When Frank L. West graduated from the Utah Agricultural College, he went to the University of Chicago to earn a doctor of philosophy degree in physics. In his day there was only one branch of the Church there, and it was difficult to reach from where he lived. So young Brother West decided to study the scriptures on his own. He was not reading them to prepare a speech or to defend the faith. His only desire was study for its own sake, to find out what the scriptures contained that was of interest and of value to him.

The scriptures awakened in him a genuine interest in religion. He became a highly effective Sunday School teacher of college students. President Heber J. Grant called him to be the LDS Commissioner of Education. Throughout his life, he referred frequently to the same passages of scripture he had marked in Chicago.

Frank West was childlike in his curiosity, in his avid search for the meaning of the gospel in human experience. His faith in the gospel, richly nourished in his youth by the study of scripture, sustained him through his scientific studies and the vicissitudes of life.

The scriptures can mean as much to you. Make your own ready-reference. Keep a large loose-leaf notebook beside your standard works and, as you come to a passage on a vital subject such as faith, for instance, list it under the topic *Faith*. Annotate the passage briefly. For example: Alma 32—describes how faith grows, what happens when it is neglected, and what its fruits are.

Another title might be forgiveness and would include such great statements as found in the following chapters:

> *Forgiveness.*
> Ezekiel 18—powerful, detailed assurance of complete forgiveness following true repentance.
> Luke 15—Jesus' beautiful parables on the lost sheep, the lost coin, and the lost (prodigal) son.

List only the passages that have real meaning for you.

2. *Read the scriptures regularly,* each day for fifteen or thirty minutes. Don't worry if some passages are beyond

your grasp. Consult a teacher, a commentary, or return again in another year. The fault may not be in the scripture, but in your own understanding.

Read the scriptures over and over again. They become new books each time because of what life does to us. The scriptures do not change; we bring different eyes and minds to them. Even though I have read all of the standard works many times, I am always surprised at my discoveries on each reading.

3. *Read the scriptures thoughtfully as you do any other book.* Read them with an alert, critical mind, making sure that you understand what you are reading.

But be more than rational, more than critical. The scriptures are to be read in humility, with reverence, with a desire to have the Holy Spirit as an interpreter. The scriptures should be read in the same spirit in which they were written by men who were often "moved upon by the Holy Ghost."

Read them to learn the will of God and the true values of life.

4. A final warning: *Do not take pride in your knowledge of scripture and become dogmatic in your interpretations.* Take the scriptures seriously, but not yourself too seriously. Enjoy the scriptures in all their humanity and divinity. Remain open-minded, eager to learn, receptive to new insights, remembering the admonition of Jesus:

"Ask, and it shall be given you; seek, and ye shall find; knock, and it shall be opened unto you." (Matthew 7:7.)

Index